Who is Lulu? What

Lulu is all things and something different to every man.

She is fact, she is myth; she is corporeal, she is idea; she is realist, she is ideal.

Lulu is the eternal-womanly that draws us downward.

Not even her name is an ascertainable fact. . . . Nor does she have a definite past. . . .

She is nothing and all; she is being without mind, without thought, without conscience: she is not merely demonic, she is demon personified.

Lulu is the "wild and true and beautiful beast" . . . the incarnation of sexual desire and instinct.

But Lulu is innocent . . . the flame that lures a moth with its light, and which is destroyed in the flame's primal heat. She seeks no sacrifice: the moths . . . come of their own volition, and each in turn is destroyed.

From the Introduction by
Carl Richard Mueller

This series, devoted to both the classic and modern theatre, to playwrights both known and neglected, has been designed as a prompt to performance. Plays exist within a historical frame and the repertory naturally changes over the years. From time to time it is good to refresh the repertory by rescuing from neglect some plays which may not have pleased yesterday's taste but which seem well-suited to our own. And there are new plays which demand early translation into English. We hope this series will serve both purposes.

—Richard Schechner
General Editor,
Tulane Drama Review Series

FRANK WEDEKIND

THE LULU PLAYS

Earth Spirit
Pandora's Box
Death and the Devil

Newly Translated and with an Introduction by
CARL RICHARD MUELLER

A FAWCETT PREMIER BOOK
Fawcett Publications, Inc., Greenwich, Conn.
Member of American Book Publishers Council, Inc.

Library of Congress Catalog Card Number: 67-20947

First Fawcett Premier printing, April 1967

Published by Fawcett World Library,
67 West 44th Street, New York, New York 10036

Printed in the United States of America

FOR

WILLIAM W. MELNITZ

On the Occasion of His Retirement
And in Honor of a Life devoted to
Scholarship and the Theater
With Kindest Regards

—C. R. M.

Contents

Wedekind and the Morality of the Flesh

I: Overview

Frank Wedekind, German dramatist, born 1864, died 1918, lived one of the most colorful lives, as well as one of the most contradictory, of modern times. A man uprooted from almost his earliest days, he wandered the world in the company of adventurers, libertines, perverts, and underground figures of mystery and intrigue. He has been called one of the major forces in modern drama for the influence he exerted in breaking up the bathos of neoromanticism as well as the stolidity of naturalism. He was in fact a vital forerunner of the subjective, uninhibited, and psychologically fragmented movement known as expressionism, and is regarded as being a direct forebear of our contemporary Theater of the Absurd. He was the first to lash out against the hypocrisy of the bourgeois world in the last decade of the 19th century; and he began a violent attack on the sexual mores of the Bismarckian Age. He is rightly called the prophet of sexuality in modern drama. Society's antagonism toward the power of sex is the motivating force in the entire body of his work. And yet, Wedekind was a moralist in the strictest sense of the word. In the three "Lulu" plays contained in this volume he shows not merely the freedom of the sexual force, but the tragedy inherent in its destructiveness. Sex, he seems to say, is its own enemy. Nonetheless he championed its liberation. We see its tragedy in the demise of Lulu, and in the mortally disillusioned figure of the author in the last of the three plays.

A total antinaturalist, Wedekind's plays gain much of their power from their greater-than-life figures, the overdrawn, the grotesque, and the often savagely caricatured characters and situations. In many ways he is the link between the brilliant early 19th century German playwright Georg Büchner and the contemporary avant-gardists from Beckett to Ionesco and beyond.

II: The Early Life

Frank Wedekind is undoubtedly one of the giants of modern drama. If today his contribution tends to be taken for granted, it is because his work and its effects were so thorough that they have become one with us. We fail to see them for the very fact that they are so overwhelmingly present.

Wedekind was a moralist. Yet he was modern in the sense that his concept of morality was divided; he was torn between two divergent poles of life and thought: the conventional bourgeois morality on the one hand, and the new morality of sexual freedom and liberation on the other. The latter was his personal contribution to the way of the world, a world that in his day lay under the pall of sexual hypocrisy and repression, a world in which one thing was preached and another was desired.

In Frank Wedekind the desire for the expression of the repressed self was unnaturally strong; yet the bourgeois pall of commonplace morality was always with him, nagging and eating away at his conscience. Like the triumphant but tormented men of the Elizabethan Renaissance, and like his fellow countryman and nature, Johannes Faustus, Wedekind had two souls burning in his breast. It was one soul that furnished the impetus to express himself; and the other that rebelled against this and was his eternal torment.

Born in Germany in 1864, Frank Wedekind's life from almost its inception was one of uprootedness.

His father was a German liberal and supporter of the 1848 Revolution, a doctor who wanted to establish an orthopedic clinic and watering-place but who, after a short time as a practical physician, migrated to Constantinople, joined the Turkish service, and traveled with various expeditions to the Tigris and Euphrates Rivers. Three years later he went from Palermo to Rome to Paris, which latter he found so agreeable that he remained there until the autumn of 1847.

Disenchanted with the Revolution of 1848 in its attempts at democratic action, he repaired to North America, where he settled as a doctor in San Francisco. Here he met and married a young actress from the local German-speaking theater who was almost half his age. Two years later, in

1864, they returned to Europe, where their second child, named Benjamin Franklin, in honor of the land of freedom that harbored them, was born. Once in Hannover, Frank's father, a man independently wealthy, retired from his medical practice and gave himself over to politics. His disgust with Bismarck and his new Reich drove the Wedekind family to Switzerland in 1872.

In Switzerland Frank and his brother Armin lived a reasonably happy childhood in Schloss Lenzburg in Canton Aargau. Because of the family's liberal tendencies, the Wedekind children were tutored privately and in boarding schools.

Frank was to have become a lawyer but forced permission to take a semester of literature and art courses. He matriculated at the University of Lausanne. In 1884 he and his brother went to Munich, a city that was to remain central for most of Wedekind's life.

1886 found him working as publicity agent for a soup manufacturing firm near Zurich. It was here he made the acquaintance of the young socialist-naturalist group of writers, among whom were Carl and Gerhart Hauptmann. Yet Wedekind had no leanings, even at that early date, toward the dull and photographic observation that was the religion of the naturalists. His interest lay not with the Fourth Estate of workers, but with the mysterious underworld, with the adventurers, the drifters, and artists, with asocial types, and children.

Wedekind and Hauptmann became enemies as a result of Hauptmann's breaking a personal confidence imparted to him by Wedekind regarding the latter's unhappy parental family life brought about by the separation of his parents and the effects such experiences have on the children involved. This information was worked by Hauptmann into his play *Das Friedensfest*. Wedekind retaliated with a satiric comedy in which he ridiculed the photographic realism of the naturalist school.

One salutary thing, however, did emerge from the meeting of these two men and writers. It was Wedekind's good fortune to be introduced by Hauptmann to the long-neglected and only recently rediscovered early 19th-century playwright and revolutionary Georg Büchner. This introduction to Büchner's works furnished the young Wedekind with the stylistic basis upon which to found his future work: fragmented dialogue, frenetic, episodic scenes, a distortion of natural phenomena to arrive at the true center, and the disarmingly modern technique of isolation as seen in the tendency of characters to talk past rather than at one another.

While his naturalist brethren worked at their trade of observation, Wedekind spent six months wandering from country to country with a circus troupe. London, Paris, Munich, Leipzig, Berlin, Silesia, Switzerland, Austria, and Southern Germany—these were the places he visited, and where he wrote his first short sketches and stories.

III: Spring's Awakening

In 1891 Frank Wedekind published his first book, a tragedy of childhood entitled *Spring's Awakening*, which he had written between autumn of 1890 and Easter 1891. It was a trailblazer in many respects. In the first place, it inaugurated a new kind of drama — what was soon to be termed expressionism; and secondly, it spoke out loudly and yet with tender love and compassion regarding the trials and torments accompanying the sexual awakening of puberty. Because of the moral repression and prudery of his time, its hypocrisy and bourgeois smugness, *Spring's Awakening* met with violent antagonism and censorship. The play was not performed until 1906, and then only in a bowdlerized version.

The most startling and disturbing fact to his fellow human beings was that he should flout morality and decency and the long-accepted and time-honored standards of the bourgeois establishment. Wedekind was saying to them that nature cannot lie, that nature is truth, and therefore nature is morality. In repressing its sexual instincts, he maintained, his age was poisoning itself; natural instincts were regarded as sinful; the people of the time were subjugating naked beauty and enslaving its youth. To Wedekind nakedness and beauty and truth were one and the same: the triune unity of his universe.

Spring's Awakening is the story of adolescence at the time when the sexual urge is experienced for the first time; at a time when it is still mysterious and frightening and wonderful — confusion and elation being strangely intermingled. The crux of the play is the opposition the child meets from his elders at the moment when openness and understanding are most needed.

Wedekind's children in this play, Wendla, Melchior and Moritz, are naïve, and it is from this naïveté that much of the beauty of this play derives. Their dialogue served as a fresh breath of lyricism in the stuffy atmosphere of its time. Wedekind shows these children caught up in their overwhelming dilemma.

MORITZ: I've got a question —

MELCHIOR: Well?

MORITZ: Will you answer me?

MELCHIOR: Of course.

MORITZ: The truth?

MELCHIOR: Shake hands on it? — Well, what is it, Moritz?

* * *

MORITZ: Have you felt it yet?

MELCHIOR: What?

MORITZ: How did you put it?

MELCHIOR: Feelings of manhood?

MORITZ: M-hm.

MELCHIOR: Of course.

MORITZ: Me, too.

MELCHIOR: I've known about it for a long time. Almost a year now.

MORITZ: I felt like . . . like a bolt of lightning hit me.

And later in the same scene:

MORITZ: Melchior, did you ever try to think how we ever got into this terrible-wonderful mess?

MELCHIOR: You mean you don't know?

MORITZ: How should I? I know how hens lay eggs, and they say mother's supposed to have carried me under her heart. But is that enough? —— I still remember when I was five years old, how I got embarrassed whenever anybody turned up the Queen of Hearts with her dress cut clear down to here. Well, that feeling went away. But today it's all I can do to talk to a girl anymore without thinking about something disgusting. And I swear, Melchior, I don't know *what*. . . . I've gone through *Meyers Little Encyclopedia* from A to Z. Words — nothing but words! Not a single explanation! My God, and the shame that goes with it! What's the use of having an encyclopedia that doesn't answer the most obvious questions in the world?

To Wendla's questions about where her married sister's new baby has come from, her mother at first advances the stork-reply; and then:

WENDLA: Here I have a sister who's been married two and a half years, and I'm an aunt for the third time, and I haven't the faintest idea how it all happens. —— Don't be angry with me, Mother, don't be angry. You're the only person in the world I can ask. Please, Mother, please tell me. Please tell me. I'm even ashamed of myself. Please, Mother, say something. And don't scold me for asking. Answer me — how does it happen? I'm fourteen years old — how can you still want me to believe in the stork!

MRS. BERGMAN: Good Heavens, child, how strange you are. — The things you think of. — I couldn't begin such a thing.

Then, after repeated pleading by Wendla, her mother finally does her best:

MRS. BERGMAN: In order to have a child — a person must — must *love* the man she's married to — yes, she must *love* him — as one can only love a man. She must love him so completely, with all her heart, that — that it can't be spoken of. She must love him, Wendla, in a way which you at your age are quite incapable of loving . . . — So now you know.

The moral cowardice of parents that Wedekind is indicting here results in Wendla's quite innocently becoming pregnant and her death at the hands of an abortionist brought in furtively by her uncomprehending mother.

The school and the teacher also come under fire, and Wedekind typifies the latter as a near-babbling idiot. The language of the parents in the play is extremely earthbound and prosaic; the language of the teacher, the German pedant, is reduced to virtual nonsense and numb hardheadedness.

All of which contrasts greatly with the simple, natural lyricism of the children's dialogue.

Moritz commits suicide by shooting out his brains because he failed to be promoted and was ashamed of the disgrace his parents would feel. Melchior is tried by his teachers for having written a tract on copulation for Moritz, to satisfy his natural curiosity. Melchior flees the reformatory into which his parents have placed him, because, says his father,

MR. GABOR: He'll find there, above all else, what was unjustly withheld from him at home: iron discipline, principles, and moral constraint, to which under all circumstances he must submit. — Besides, the reformatory isn't so terrible a place as you may think. Its main emphasis is on developing Christian thought and feeling. The boy will at long last be instructed to desire what is good rather than what is *interesting*, and to direct his actions towards that which is sanctioned by *law*.

Here is Wedekind's most explicit statement regarding the sin of parents against children: insistence on the death of the natural instinct and desire. These men, these demons, parents and teachers and society as a whole, Wedekind draws in various degrees of distortion and caricature. They are the evil spirits he is trying to exorcise.

In the final scenes of *Spring's Awakening*, Wedekind introduces himself in the guise of the Muffled Gentleman, the Man in the Mask. The scene is a graveyard; it is night and the wind blows both sky and earth. The ghost of Moritz appears carrying his head in his arms, and meets Melchior just escaped from the reformatory. Moritz tries to lure Melchior into taking his hand and thus joining him in the world of the dead. But each time Melchior instinctively declines. At the crucial moment, the Man in the Mask, Wedekind, the Spirit of Life, appears and, wrapping Melchior in his arms, restores him to the world of the living, to life, beauty, truth — nature.

Wedekind's intention is clear, and he shows the way to sanity as no one before him had done. The convention of hypocrisy must fall to the trumpet blast of innocence and truth. To be sure, this is naïve — but not all that unattainable. Wedekind was never again to present his theme so freshly, so sympathetically, and so tenderly as he did in *Spring's Awakening*.

IV: The Darker Vision

From this point onward to the end of his life Wedekind's view of life and sexuality changed — or, if not precisely changed, then at least grew more intensely perverse. He set out to deliberately sexualize the world, to turn its eyes toward the truth. To do this most efficiently he gave himself over to the kind of life his major later works were to mirror.

Artur Kutscher, Wedekind's chief biographer, remarks that during Wedekind's sojourn in Paris from 1891 through 1893 he sought to know love in all its manifestations. His diaries were filled to overflowing with the names of prostitutes with whom he whiled away his days and nights. Casanova might well have served as example.

And yet this life was scarcely new. Rather he revelled in the conventional modern decadence of such figures as Baudelaire, Verlaine, Rimbaud, and Oscar Wilde: a life of excess in every respect. He gave himself over to debauchery and perversion to the point of near exhaustion, till finally he collapsed into horrible periods of extended sleep. It was precisely this life that he was soon to illustrate in his "Lulu" plays, *Earth Spirit* and *Pandora's Box.*

Wedekind at one time sought desperately to unite two opposites — opposite at least in the mind of his time — two esthetics: the Flesh and the Spirit. Man must be more than a dust-eating worm. It could not be that man must lay in the bonds of the flesh — not wholly, at any rate. He must be more than a slave to the flesh; for, after all, he was the master of the world in and through that same flesh. For such a man wings were more proper than chains. But Wedekind was met with arrogant arguments to the contrary and was afraid that the pairing of these opposites would succumb before the onslaught. Therefore he proclaimed his more radical discovery: the Morality of the Flesh. In a programmatic essay entitled *On Eroticism,* he maintained that the flesh is in possession of its own spirit; it is its own esthetic; the spirit of the flesh is the flesh's lust. This, then, is the central theme of his "Lulu" plays, and of *Earth Spirit* in particular.

V: The "Lulu" Plays

Who is Lulu? What is she?

Lulu is all things and something different to every man. She is fact, she is myth; she is corporeal, she is idea; she is realist, she is ideal.

Lulu is the eternal-womanly that draws us downward. Not even her name is an ascertainable fact. For her first husband, Goll, she is Nelly; for her second husband, Schwarz, she is Eve; for Dr. Schoen, her third husband, she is Mignon; and for Schigolch, her "father," she is Lulu. Nor does she have a definite past. Schigolch is perhaps her father, but neither we nor anyone else know for certain. She tells Schoen that her father died in an asylum. But:

RODRIGO: Then she's not your daughter?

SCHIGOLCH: Never occurs to her.

HUGENBERG: Then what's her father's name?

SCHIGOLCH: She's bragged about me.

HUGENBERG: Then what's her father's name?

SCHIGOLCH: What did he say?

RODRIGO: What's her father's name?

SCHIGOLCH: She never had one.

Regarding her mother, Schoen says: "She never knew her mother — not to mention where her grave is. — Her mother doesn't have a grave."

She is nothing and all; she is being without mind, without thought, without conscience: she is not merely demonic, she is demon personified.

SCHWARZ: Just one question . . .

LULU: I can't answer you.

SCHWARZ: Can you tell the truth?

LULU: I don't know.

SCHWARZ: Do you believe in a Creator?

LULU: I don't know.

SCHWARZ: Is there anything you can swear by?

LULU: I don't know. Leave me alone! You've lost your mind!

SCHWARZ: What *do* you believe in?

LULU: I don't know.

SCHWARZ: Do you have a soul?

LULU: I don't know.

SCHWARZ: Have you ever been in love?

LULU: I don't know.

SCHWARZ (*rises, walks to the left; to himself*): She doesn't know!

LULU (*without moving*): I don't know.

Lulu is the "wild and true and beautiful beast" that Wedekind speaks of in his Prologue to *Earth Spirit*. She is elusive as the snake, the form in which she is first introduced to us in the Prologue. She is primal force — the incarnation of sexual desire and instinct. Yet her motivating force is ego; for love, to Wedekind, is not altruistic but egoistic; and Lulu's entire being is directed at one thing: self-fulfillment.

The most frustrating fact about Lulu is that she never offers, she never tries, she never has to solicit. For the most part she is a passive creature; passive in that she needs only to exist as the flame of a candle exists, shifting and twisting and turning, never the same twice, alluring and luring, enticing, ensnaring. But: *Innocent*. Despite her draw, she does not ply her trade, for she has none save living, existence, experience. And all this comes to her by force of nature. Lulu, then, is innocent of the horror she brings in her wake. She is no more guilty than the flame that lures a moth with its light, and which is destroyed in the flame's primal heat. She seeks no sacrifice: the moths, her husbands, come of their own volition, and each in turn is destroyed.

It appears, at times, that she is quite the contrary of the voluptuary. She can be cold and inhumanly impersonal, as to Schwarz, in act one of *Earth Spirit:*

SCHWARZ: How do you feel?

LULU: As if I'd fallen in water . . .

SCHWARZ: I love you.

LULU: I loved a student once.

SCHWARZ: Nelly . . .

LULU: He had twenty-four dueling scars . . .

SCHWARZ: I love you, Nelly.

LULU: My name is not Nelly.

(SCHWARZ *kisses her.*)

LULU: My name is Lulu.

SCHWARZ: I shall call you Eve.

LULU: Do you know what time it is?

SCHWARZ (*looking at the clock*): Half-past ten.

(LULU *takes the clock and opens the case.*)

SCHWARZ: You don't love me.

LULU: Oh, but I do . . . It's a few minutes after half-past ten.

SCHWARZ: Kiss me, Eve!

LULU (*takes him by the chin and kisses him; throws the clock in the air and catches it*): You smell of tobacco.

SCHWARZ: Why don't you call me by my first name?

LULU: I'd feel uncomfortable.

SCHWARZ: You're being a hypocrite.

LULU: It seems *you're* the hypocrite. — I? Hypocritical? Whatever made you say that? — I've *never* needed that.

Once Schwarz has slit his throat in desperation over his life with Lulu, Lulu says to those present, just after the suicide, when asked what she will tell the police:

LULU: Nothing.

ALVA: He wanted to give back to Fate precisely what she gave him.

LULU: His first thoughts were always of murder.

ALVA: He possessed what most people only dream of!

LULU: He paid dearly for it, too.

Lulu is also the super-realist. Her retorts are almost always disarmingly practical but also distanced, impersonal, cold, rational, and unpremeditated. Perhaps it is not too far wrong to say that her very draw is that same coldness, distance, and disinterest; for she shows no sign of love for any man. She incites desire, but she never gives. Her existence is to take, to absorb. She is the epitome of ego. A one-sided selfish creature.

She is also more than a voluptuary—she is almost self-sufficient. "When she dances her solo," remarks Prince Escerny, "she becomes intoxicated with her own beauty—she seems mortally in love with it." And later:

ESCERNY: Imagine if instead of that rabble out there you had only *one* spectator, a *chosen* one.

LULU: It wouldn't make any difference. I never see anyone anyway.

Yet she is not wholly self-sufficient:

LULU: Looking at myself in the mirror I wished I were a man . . . my own husband.—

ALVA: You envy even your husband the happiness you offer him.

She cares little for others and has no interest in understanding another's inner being. "When he's drunk," says Schigolch of Schwarz, "you can see straight into his insides." And she: "I'd prefer not to." Later in the same scene he remarks: "But I'm still deeply sensitive to the things of this world." And Lulu: "I'm not."

SCHIGOLCH: What are you now?

LULU: An animal . . .

But a moment following she admits to pampering herself:

SCHIGOLCH: We're nothing but dust.

LULU: I beg your pardon! I rub myself with oil, and powder everyday.

SCHIGOLCH: Probably worth it, too, for that coxcomb's sake.

LULU: It makes my skin feel like satin.

SCHIGOLCH: As though it were still anything less than dirt.

LULU: Thank you. But I'd like to be good enough to eat.

One of the key statements in *Earth Spirit* is Lulu's announcement that she cannot love by command. Up to this point we have seen how such a thing would be impossible for her, would mean her death. She is incapable of making a living off of love, because her life *is* love. She exhibits disgust toward prostitution, for to engage in so common a practice would be to violate her very nature. In *Pandora's Box* she finds herself at her lowest ebb, when she says: "I want to cut off my hands for having sinned so against my judgment;" and: "Is there anything sadder in this world than a lady of pleasure!" And then, when faced with the portrait of herself made at the time of her true self, she screams out in disgust at the contrast between the picture and herself at that moment: "Monster! What did you bring it *here* for! —Get it out of my sight! Throw it out the window!" And when Schigolch in the final scene of the same play eggs her on to go out and walk her beat, Lulu cries out: "You're killing me! I can't bear it!"

Lulu is a free and unfettered spirit; to tie her down, to cause her to sell what she must merely radiate and dispense with as though it were God-given grace, without thought or meditation, is to violate the instinctual element of her nature, and that is tantamount to total destruction. She says this most explicitly in the second act of *Pandora's Box*, when Casti-Piani, the white-slave trader, tries to blackmail her into a house of prostitution:

LULU: A woman like myself could never be happy in a house like that. It might have pleased me when I was fifteen. At that time I doubted I'd ever be happy. I bought a revolver; and at night ran barefoot across the bridge to the park to shoot myself in the snow. Then I had the good fortune of lying in the hospital for three months without ever seeing a man. It was then my eyes opened and I saw myself as I really was. Night after night I dreamt of the man I was made for and who was made for me. Then when I was set loose again upon men, I was no longer a silly goose. Ever since, I've been able to tell in the dead of night and at a hundred paces whether a man and I are made for each other. And if I find I've sinned against my judgment, the next day I feel soiled both inside and out, and it takes weeks to overcome my loathing for myself. And here you are, thinking I'll throw myself at every no-good so-and-so.

Earth Spirit, then, is a hymn to the untrammeled, instinctual life, glorified in that mystery that is Lulu on the rise to her personal zenith. In that play, however, her last action is to perform what may well be the first action in her life. She takes life into her hands and voluntarily extinguishes it when she deliberately shoots and kills her third husband, Dr. Schoen. As she says herself, he is the only man she ever loved, and we may well take this to be a true statement, for he was a taskmaster who ruled her with a whip. Yet this is the man she kills, the only man who ever stood up to her, at least for a time, and gave her a hard time; and for this she respected him. In killing Schoen, however, she does not merely violate the law, but also, as it were, loses control of her very being. She makes herself vulnerable to others. Her past innocence lay on the foundations of her inaction. But now she has suddenly and irrevocably turned the tables on herself. Her act, her first act in life, has for the first time brought her within the reach of her society, the very ones she once controlled merely by her presence.

In the second play we see the working out of this tragic error, this error that propelled her beyond the limits of her being. She is steadily, act by act, seen to be on the decline. She is open to being *used* by her fellows but is unable any longer to use *them*. She might be blackmailed at any moment as a result of her escape from prison. Rodrigo is going to make a fabulous trapeze artist of her and be a rich man; Casti-Piani is going to sell her to an expensive house of prostitution in Cairo; and, in the final act of the play, in the filthy, dismal London attic, damp with rain dripping in through the skylight, Schigolch and Alva actually do prostitute her services to bring in the little they need to stay alive. In submitting she violates both her nature and her judgment, and this leads to the only alternative: death.

This uncompromising demise of Lulu and what she stands for can be seen in only one light insofar as Wedekind is concerned; namely the destructiveness inherent in the free sexual instinct. This may seem odd when viewed in regard to the pristine life-giving joyous element of sex as seen in *Spring's Awakening*. Yet we must give ear to Wedekind's own existence, to the primness and bourgeois precision of his surface life and appearance, and the undeniable freedom of his inner, personal life. His biographers have stressed this polarity sufficiently, and there is no need to draw it out to any great length here.

It has been suggested, and probably rightly, that Wedekind the sexual liberator was so much the traditional moralist that, following the orgy, he was attacked by the furies of his bourgeois conscience. His involvement with the exterior tradition of the bourgeois world and life demanded the gigantic denouement to the Lulu orgy, which is *Pandora's Box:* the descent into hell without promise of resurrection, the pay-off. But then, too, Wedekind maintained that he was devoted to the truth. In *The Censor* he proclaimed that the truth was always before him, that he never falsified reality. Perhaps his life in foreign capitals, luxuriating in debauchery and perversion, taught him precisely this: that excess inevitably pays the consequences. Perhaps the tension we attribute to the pull of the two poles, sensuality and prudish morality, was less a factor of his divided life than Wedekind's greater wisdom, derived from not merely observing life but actually involving himself in the very life he wrote about: his words being the mirror of this experience, which is to say the truth. This is perhaps strengthened by the fact that Wedekind sensed, actually lived, the perverted, abandoned life; and feeling himself in a way a perversion of the perverse, that is to say normal, he could put in the mouth of the most obviously perverted individual in the whole work, the Countess Geschwitz, the lesbian lover of Lulu, the only truly clear, and the most explicit, view of the human condition in the entire work. She is an outcast and scorned, a truly pitiable figure, one who has absorbed the true knowledge by virtue of being severed from not only the perverse life of cosmopolitan society, but from the normal one as well. In the final pages of the great dying fall which is act three of *Pandora's Box* she says as she sits alone in the dismal attic:

GESCHWITZ: I'll sit beside the door. I'll watch it all and not move an eyelash. (*She sits on the cane chair beside the door.*) — People don't know each other — they have no idea what they're like. The only ones who know them are those who aren't human themselves. Every word they utter is untrue, a lie. But they don't know that, because today they're this and tomorrow that, and it all depends on whether or not they've eaten, drunk, and loved. Only the body remains constant for a time, and only children have any understanding. Men and women are like animals; not one of them knows what he's doing. At their happiest moments they moan and groan, and in moments of deepest misery they delight in the slightest trifle. It's amazing how hunger deprives men of the strength to withstand misfortune. But when they've gorged themselves they turn the world into a torture-chamber, and throw lives away to satisfy a whim. — I wonder if there have ever been people who have found happiness in love. — What is happiness to them, but sleeping better and being able to forget others. — I'm not a human being; my body has nothing in common with human bodies. And yet I have a human soul. The tormented have within them a narrow, shrivelled soul; but I know I have nothing to gain by giving away and sacrificing everything . . .

Possibly we can never really understand the true nature of the two souls that existed in the body of Frank Wedekind; yet we cannot fail to see the direction his life and thought took very early in his artistic career. We can profitably contrast the figures of the Man in the Mask of *Spring's Awakening*, the spirit of the life force, of sex, of being in its pristine, lovely, lyrical form, and the death figure, the negation of life, the figure representative of the curse of the uninhibited, abandoned life, the character of the sex-murderer Jack the Ripper who finally disembowels Lulu, thus bringing to a fitting close Wedekind's dark vision of sexuality and its consequences.

VI: Epilogue: Death and the Devil

In the final play, which has some connection with the actual "Lulu" plays, *Death and the Devil*, we see what we must take to be a fictionalized but true picture of Wedekind's final thoughts on the life represented in the "Lulu" plays.

Casti-Piani, who appears in *Pandora's Box* as a man of twenty-five or so, is here seen to be a man of sixty or more. Like Wedekind, he has preached the life of sexual freedom. He is a white-female-slave trader and believes that his profession has helped innumerable women to find and fulfill their natures. His view of the life force is total sensual pleasure as the highest gift of life. He is nothing short of a romantic moralist, as was Wedekind, who rejects everything but total liberation of the senses. Without this belief, he says, he would have committed suicide fifty years ago.

And yet what happens in the course of *Death and the Devil?* Two conversions are brought about. The prim and respectable virginal opponent of Casti-Piani's views, Elfriede von Malcus, is converted to the side of Casti-Piani, for she sees the truly sacrificial nature of prostitution; whereas Casti-Piani is shown the delusion he has suffered under the entire length of his days.

To convince Elfriede of the nobility of the life he has fostered all these years he arranges for the two of them to overhear a meeting between a male customer and one of Casti-Piani's girls. In the course of this conversation, he learns of the terrible burden and torment suffered as a result of the sensual life.

Mr. King, the customer, eventually understands what the girl is trying to convince him of:

MR. KING: I see it revealed as blinding clear as the sun:
That even in this house there is no peace
For the senses.

And the girl, Lisiska:

LISISKA: No, you mustn't leave me! Listen to me!
I was an innocent child and began
My life with seriousness, zeal and duty.
Untroubled laughter never became me.
I heard not only my teachers, but my brothers and sisters
Whisper about me in an awesome way;
And even my parents said to me:
One day you'll be the joy of our old age.
Then suddenly the cock crew
And all was past!
Once desire was awakened in me
It grew beyond all bounds
Beyond all thought
Beyond the true feelings of my heart
Until I was amazed at what had happened
At what had made me such a fool
Had made me not see the lightning in Heaven
Nor hear the thunder tumbled down from Heaven.
I believed, I hoped that life was given us
For inextinguishable joy.

MR. KING: And didn't you find your hope had been fulfilled? ——

I'm speaking, of course, as a blind man speaks of colors . . .

LISISKA: No — only this infernal urge
That left no room for joy.

She describes her profession as deception, false, and hollow:

LISISKA: For God's sake, you must never trust my love!
My duty here is to pretend at love.
Consider for a moment what it means
When suddenly the door is torn open
And all at once you must scrape your love together:
There stands a man: God created him. —
Would you like for me to begin this dreadful game
With you?
Only to feel disgust at your
Height of bliss?
And yet if with your sturdy peasant's fists
You would chastise my body, and find joy
In doing so, it would bind us together till death.

And finally she confesses:

LISISKA: To all who gather here
Love is eternal torment,
Insatiable greed. . . .
How long my dream of highest bliss has been
A land of undisturbed eternal rest!
If only I could die beneath your fists!

Casti-Piani's life is destroyed. His life has been wasted, has lost his purpose. He should have shot himself fifty years ago.

CASTI-PIANI: What's there left for me when sensual pleasure is only hellish human slaughter, when sensual pleasure is only satanic human slaughter, like all the rest of earth! So this is that ray of divine light that penetrates the dreadful midnight of our martyr's existence. I wish I'd put a bullet through my head fifty years ago! Then I'd have been spared admitting this miserable bankruptcy of my swindling, stolen-together spirituality!

I think we may accept this as the darkest statement and realization of Wedekind's life. The only difference being that he never quite gave up trying to prove that it wasn't really so.

CARL RICHARD MUELLER

University of California
Los Angeles

EARTH SPIRIT

A Tragedy in Four Acts

CAST OF CHARACTERS

DOCTOR GOLL
DOCTOR SCHOEN, editor-in-chief
ALVA, his son
SCHWARZ, an artist
PRINCE ESCERNY, an African explorer
SCHIGOLCH
RODRIGO, an acrobat
HUGENBERG, a schoolboy
ESCHERICH, a reporter
LULU
COUNTESS GESCHWITZ, an artist
FERDINAND, a coachman
HENRIETTE, a chambermaid
A FOOTMAN

PROLOGUE

The curtain rises to reveal the entrance to a tent. Accompanied by sounds of clashing cymbals and the beating of drums, an ANIMAL TRAINER *enters. He is dressed in a vermillion frockcoat, white tie, white breeches and top boots. His hair is long, black, and wiry. He carries a riding-whip and a loaded revolver.*

Proud Gentlemen and Ladies who love pleasure,
Step right up and enter our little zoo!
Behold with sensual eyes and horror too
The soulless creatures of our little crew,
Brought to their knees by human genius' measure.
Step right up! The show is about to begin! —
One child is admitted free with a pair of his kin.

You'll see man and beast fight in a narrow cage:
The one swings his whip with high disdain,
The other roars, and with murderous rage
Descends upon the man he cannot contain.
First cleverness and then strength wins the day;
First man then beast lies stretched upon the clay.
The beast rears up, and man falls down and squeals!
And yet, a cold and domineering glance
Lays low the beast in his downward advance,
Which piously accepts the conqueror's heels.

Times are bad!—All those Ladies and Gentlemen
Who once would throng about my little cage
Now honor farces, dramas, operas, Ibsen,
Bestowing their presence on them with a rage.
My hungry pensioners are low on feed,
And so they devour each other with ravening greed.

Oh, for the life of an actor who's employed!
He's always certain his bones will not lack cover,
No matter how low above others hunger may hover;
Or how great in his colleagues' stomachs may be the void.
Yet, if you care to do great things in your day,
You must never equate merit with its pay.

What do these sad and happy plays reveal?—
Domestic beasts, well-mannered in all they feel,
Who cool their rage on a vegetarian meal,
And revel in shedding a comfortable tear,
Like those out there—trembling in cosy fear.
This hero doesn't know how to hold his liquor,
That one is uncertain of his love,
And a third one with the world has begun to bicker;
And for five long acts he grows sicker and sicker,
With no one around to send him off Above.—
Gentlemen! Ladies! — Only through me alone
May the wild and true and beautiful beast be shown.
You see the tiger, who, according to habit,
Strikes down whatever comes within its path.
You see the bear that gulps down too much rabbit,
And after a late dinner dies in his bath.
And then there is the charming little monkey
That passes its time in boredom for all to see;
He has talent, and yet seems lacking in greatness,
And so he openly coquettes with his nakedness.
By my soul, you'll see inside my tent
A camel standing directly behind this rent!—
These beasts crouch silently around my feet,
When — (*he shoots into the audience*) — my revolver suddenly resounds.
The creatures tremble; I stay cool — on the grounds
That man stays cool — in order that I may greet
You.

Enter! — What's this! You won't budge yourselves?
Well then, you may be the judge yourselves!
You see reptiles here from all regions:
Chameleons, snakes, dragons and crocodiles,
Salamanders that live in clefts, and legions
Of other slimy things. What's that? You smile?
You swear you won't believe a word I say?

(He lifts the tentflap and calls inside.)

August! Ho! Bring the snake this way!

(A paunchy WORKER *carries from the tent the actress playing* LULU, *dressed in her Pierrot costume, and sets her down in front of the* ANIMAL TRAINER.*)*

She was created to stir up great disaster,
To lure, seduce, and poison, to be the master
Of murder, so that no one finds the traces.

(He tickles LULU *under the chin.)*

My dear, sweet creature, you mustn't pull such faces!
Be neither foolish, affected, nor perverse—
Not even when you elicit a critic's curse.
You have no right to dislocate our views
Of woman's primal form with hisses and mews;
Or by means of jests and wild devices
Bring disgust on childhood's simple vices!
You should — and therefore I speak at such great length —
Speak naturally, for therein lies your strength!
Since time began, our basic rule has meant
That every art should be self-evident!

(To the audience.)

Just now there's nothing special to be seen;
But wait awhile, and you will see what I mean.
She winds about the tiger with a powerful bend;
He howls and groans! — And who wins in the end?! —
Hurry, August! Carry her to her place! —

(The WORKER *lifts* LULU *across his arms; the* ANIMAL TRAINER *fondles her hips.)*

Oh, sweet innocence! — Oh, full of grace!

(The WORKER *carries* LULU *back into the tent.)*

And now for the real highlights of the day:
My head between the jaws of a beast of prey.
Step right up! The sight is not a new one,
And yet it always pleases when it's done.
I'll rip his jaws apart, quite without fear,

And he would never dare to cause a tear.
Lovely, wild, and varied as he may be,
Yet he treats my head with courtesy!
I trust him, put my head between his teeth:
Then once he thinks it a joke: and with his leth-
Al jaws he cracks my skull; yet carelessly
I choose to set my life at a pin's fee:
I toss the whip away, these weapons, too, ——
And stand here as God made me, innocent, new. —
Tell me, do you know this wild beast's name? ——
Well, then, my friends — come and play our game!

(The sounds of clashing cymbals and the beating of drums accompany the ANIMAL TRAINER *back into the tent.)*

ACT ONE

A spacious studio. — At the rear and to the left, the main entrance; downstage right, a sidedoor into a bedroom. At center, a platform for a model. Behind the podium, a Spanish screen. In front of the podium, a Smyrna rug. Downstage left, two easels. On the upstage one, the portrait of a girl. Leaning against the downstage easel, a reversed canvas. In front of both easels, somewhat center, an ottoman with a tiger's skin thrown across it. Against the right wall, two armchairs. A stepladder is at rear.

SCHWARZ and SCHOEN.

SCHOEN *(seated at the foot of the ottoman, studying the portrait on the rear easel)*: You know, I'm getting to know the woman from a completely different angle.

SCHWARZ *(brush and palette in hand, standing behind the ottoman)*: I have never painted anyone whose facial features changed more constantly. — It was all I could manage to maintain a single stable feature from one day to the next.

SCHOEN: (*pointing to the picture and looking at him*): Do you find that in the picture?

SCHWARZ: I talked to her during the sitting; to produce some sense of repose in her.

SCHOEN: Then I can understand the difference.

(SCHWARZ *dips the brush into the tin of oil and passes it across the portrait's features.*)

SCHWARZ: The most one can do is work as conscientiously as possible.

SCHOEN: Tell me. . .

SCHWARZ (*stepping back*): The color's turned out nicely again, too.

SCHOEN (*looking at him*): Have you ever in your life loved a woman?

SCHWARZ (*goes to the easel, dabs a bit of paint on, then steps back on the other side*): The material of the dress doesn't stand out enough yet. We don't sense there's a living, breathing body inside it.

SCHOEN: I don't doubt the work is excellent.

SCHWARZ: If you'd come over here. . .

SCHOEN (*rising*): You must have told her horror stories.

SCHWARZ: As far back as possible.

SCHOEN (*stepping backward, knocking over the canvas leaning against the downstage easel*): Excuse me. . .

SCHWARZ (*picking up the canvas*): Quite all right. . .

SCHOEN (*taken aback*): What is it?

SCHWARZ: Do you recognize her?

SCHOEN: No.

SCHWARZ: (*places the picture on the easel. It is of a woman dressed as Pierrot, holding a long shepherd's crook*): A costume picture.

SCHOEN: Now that's what I call a success!

SCHWARZ: Do you know her?

SCHOEN: No. Not in that costume, at least.

SCHWARZ: It still needs a lot of work.

SCHOEN: I suppose. . .

SCHWARZ: What can you expect? When she poses for me, I have the pleasure of conversing with her husband.

SCHOEN: Tell me. . .

SCHWARZ: About art, of course — you might say it's the culmination of my good fortune.

SCHOEN: How did you meet so charming a creature?

SCHWARZ: The way it's always done. An ancient tottering little man appears suddenly and asks if I will paint his wife. I'd accept even if she were as withered as Mother Earth herself. The next day at ten sharp, the doors fly open and old pot-belly drives this angelic creature in before him. My knees are still shaking. Then in comes a lackey, stiff as a board and in sap-green livery, with a package under his arm. Where is the dressing room? I open that door. (*He points right.*) Fortunately everything was in order. The sweet creature whisks into the room, and the old man plants himself outside it like a bulwark. Two minutes later she appears before us dressed as Pierrot. (*Shaking his head.*) I've never seen anything like it. (*He goes to the right and stares at the bedroom door.*)

SCHOEN (*who has followed him with his eyes*): And old pot-belly stands guard?

SCHWARZ (*turning around*): Her whole body was in such harmony with that impossible costume it seemed she had been born in it. She has a way of burying her arms in her pockets, and of lifting her tiny feet from the carpet — it makes the blood rush to my head when I think of it. . .

SCHOEN: That's obvious from the picture.

SCHWARZ (*shaking his head*): People like us, you know. . .

SCHOEN: Generally it's the model who talks.

SCHWARZ: She hasn't opened her mouth.

SCHOEN: Really?

SCHWARZ: Here, let me show you the costume. Just look at this material!

SCHOEN (*feeling it*): Satin.

SCHWARZ: And all in one piece.

SCHOEN: How does she get into it?

SCHWARZ: I can't really say.

SCHOEN (*holding the costume by the legs*): What enormous legs!

SCHWARZ: She pulls the left one up.

SCHOEN (*looking at the picture*): Above her knee!

SCHWARZ: And she does it enchantingly!

SCHOEN: Transparent stockings, too?

SCHWARZ: Those really take some painting!

SCHOEN: You'll manage.

SCHWARZ: And what a coquette!

SCHOEN: Why do you say that?

SCHWARZ: There are things not dreamt of in your philosophy. (*He takes the costume into the bedroom.*)

SCHOEN (*alone*): At least not while asleep. . .

SCHWARZ (*returns and looks at the clock*): If you'd like to meet her. . .

SCHOEN: No.

SCHWARZ: They should be along here any moment.

SCHOEN: How much longer will the lady be posing for you?

SCHWARZ: I'll endure these torments of Tantalus for at least another three months.

SCHOEN: I meant the other one.

SCHWARZ: I beg your pardon. Another three sittings at most. (*Accompanying him to the door.*) If only the lady would leave her blouse here. . .

SCHOEN: The pleasure was mine. I hope you'll visit me soon again. (*He collides in the doorway with* DOCTOR GOLL *and* LULU.) What in the name of Heaven!

SCHWARZ: May I introduce. . .

GOLL (*to* SCHOEN): What are you doing here?

SCHOEN (*kissing* LULU'S *hand*): My dear Mrs. Goll!

LULU: Surely you're not leaving.

GOLL: What wind blew you here?

SCHOEN: I came to see a picture of my fiancee.

LULU (*coming forward*): Your fiancee is *here?*

GOLL: So you're having work done here, too!

LULU (*in front of the portrait*): Why, look at her! How enchanting! Really charming!

GOLL (*looking around*): I suppose you've hidden her somewhere?

LULU: So this is the sweet young prodigy who's turned you into a human being!

SCHOEN: She generally sits in the afternoon.

GOLL: And you've said nothing about it?

LULU (*turning around*): Is she really as serious as all that?

SCHOEN: Shall we call it the aftereffects of finishing school, dear Madam?

GOLL (*in front of the portrait*): It's obvious you've undergone a most profound transformation.

LULU: You mustn't keep her waiting.

SCHOEN: I intend to announce our engagement in two weeks.

GOLL (*to* LULU): Let us not waste time! Hip-hop!

LULU (*to* SCHOEN): Just imagine, we drove across the new bridge at a trot. And I drove the carriage myself. (SCHOEN *tries to take his leave.*)

GOLL: Yes, of course.—We two must have a longer talk, sometime later. Hurry, Nelly! Hip-hop!

LULU: Now it's *your* turn to talk about *me*.

GOLL: Our Apelles is already licking his brushes.

LULU: I had imagined it would be much more amusing.

SCHOEN: And yet you have the endless satisfaction of providing us the most extraordinary of pleasures.

LULU (*walking to the right*): Just you wait!

SCHWARZ (*in front of the bedroom door*): If Madam would be so kind. . . (*He closes the door behind her and remains standing there.*)

GOLL: As you know, I christened her Nelly in our marriage contract.

SCHOEN: Really? — I see.

GOLL: What do you think of it?

SCHOEN: Why didn't you call her, say, Mignon?

GOLL: Well — that's an idea. I never thought of it.

SCHOEN: Do you consider names so important?

GOLL: Hm. — As you know, I have no children.

SCHOEN (*taking his cigarette-case from his pocket*): You've only been married a couple of months.

GOLL: Thank you — I don't want any.

SCHOEN: Cigarette?

GOLL (*helping himself*): This will be quite sufficient. (*To* SCHWARZ.) How's your little dancer getting along?

SCHOEN (*turning to* SCHWARZ): You and a dancer? !

SCHWARZ: The lady posed for me then only as a favor. I met her at an outing of the Saint Cecelia Society.

GOLL (*to* SCHOEN): Hm. — I think we're due for a change of weather.

SCHOEN: She seems to take her time changing.

GOLL: Not at all. She's very fast. A woman must be a virtuoso in her own calling. Just as we all must be unless we prefer to starve. (*Calling to her.*) Hip-hop, Nelly!

SCHWARZ (*at the door*): Madam!

LULU (*from inside*): Coming, coming.

GOLL (*to* SCHOEN): I simply don't understand these blockheads!

SCHOEN: I envy them. There's nothing holier to them than starvation. And they feel richer than you and I with our 30,000 Marks in dividends. Besides, you can't very well judge a person who from childhood on has lived only from palette to mouth. Why don't you help finance him? It would be a lesson in arithmetic. I lack the moral courage for such an enterprise. One can easily burn one's fingers. . .

LULU (*enters from the bedroom dressed as Pierrot*): Here I am.

SCHOEN (*turns around; after a pause*): Superb!

LULU (*comes closer*): Well?

SCHOEN: You shame the most vivid imagination!

LULU: How do you like me?

SCHOEN: A picture before which art must surely despair.

GOLL: Ah, then you agree!

SCHOEN (*to* LULU): I don't suppose you're aware of what you're doing.

LULU: Why, my duty, of course!

SCHOEN: Have you powdered yourself?

LULU: Well, really!

GOLL: She has skin so white, I've never seen its like! I've told our Raphael here to concern himself as little as possible with flesh tones. For once in my life, I can't get excited over this modernistic blotting and daubing.

SCHWARZ (*at the easel, preparing his paints*): Thanks to Impressionism modern art can take its place beside the old masters without blushing.

GOLL: I suppose if you like your art butchered, it's all right.

SCHOEN: For God's sake, don't get excited!

(LULU *throws her arms around* GOLL *and kisses him.*)

GOLL: Your chemise is showing. You must pull it in.

LULU: I'd rather not have it on at all. It only bothers me.

GOLL: He'd be just as likely to paint it as not.

LULU (*takes the shepherd's crook leaning against the Spanish screen and mounts the podium; to* SCHOEN): How would you like to stand here at attention for two hours?

SCHOEN: I'd sell my soul to the devil to change places with you.

GOLL (*sitting down at right*): Come over here. You really can see much better.

LULU (*pulling the left leg up to the knee; to* SCHWARZ): Like this?

SCHWARZ: Yes...

LULU (*pulling it a shade higher*): Hm?

SCHWARZ: Yes, yes...

GOLL (*to* SCHOEN *who has sat in the chair next to him, with* a *wave of his hand*): I find she looks even more attractive from here.

LULU (*without moving*): I beg your pardon! I'm attractive from every position!

SCHWARZ (*to* LULU): Your right knee — just a bit forward, please.

SCHOEN (*with a gesture*): Perhaps her lines are somewhat more delicate from here. . .

SCHWARZ: At least the lighting is half bearable today.

GOLL: You must get her down very quickly. Try holding your brush more towards the end.

SCHWARZ: Certainly, Doctor.

SCHOEN: Treat her as a still-life.

SCHWARZ: Certainly, Doctor. (*To* LULU.) Would you hold your head just a shade higher, Madam?

LULU (*raising her head*): Paint my lips slightly parted.

SCHOEN: Paint snow on ice. Grow warm in the process and immediately your art grows unartistic.

SCHWARZ: Certainly, Doctor!

GOLL: Art, you know, must mirror Nature so precisely that one may at least derive some *spiritual* enjoyment from it!

LULU (*parting her lips slightly; to* SCHWARZ): Like this — you see? I'll keep them half parted.

SCHWARZ: As soon as the sun gets around here, that wall outside will cast in warm reflections.

GOLL (*to* LULU): You must keep your position just as though our Velasquez here were not present.

LULU: Whatever makes you think a painter is a man!

SCHOEN: Can you draw a conclusion from a single famous exception?

SCHWARZ (*stepping back from the easel*): I wish I'd rented a new studio last fall.

SCHOEN (*to* GOLL): Tell me — have you seen little Miss O'Murphy as the Peruvian pearl-fisher?

GOLL: I'll see her tomorrow for the fourth time. Count Polossov's taking me. His hair has turned quite blond again with rapture.

SCHOEN: Then you find her as fabulous as I?

GOLL: I shouldn't want to judge beforehand!

LULU: I believe someone knocked.

SCHWARZ: Excuse me a moment. (*He goes to the door and opens it.*)

GOLL: I think you'd be safe to smile at him just a bit more freely.

SCHOEN: It wouldn't bother him in the least.

GOLL: And what if it did? — Why else do you think we're sitting here? !

ALVA SCHOEN (*still behind the Spanish screen*): May I come in?

SCHOEN: My son!

LULU: Why, it's Mr. Alva!

GOLL: Come in — no bother at all!

ALVA (*coming forward, extends his hand to* SCHOEN *and* GOLL): Doctor Goll. . . (*Turning around toward* LULU.) Do my eyes deceive me? ! If only I could still engage you as my leading lady!

LULU: Oh, I could never dance well enough for you!

ALVA: You have a dancing-master the peer of any theatre in Europe!

SCHOEN: What brings you here?

GOLL: Are you having someone painted here secretly, too?

ALVA (*to* SCHOEN): I came to take you to the dress rehearsal.

(SCHOEN *rises.*)

GOLL: Are you dancing in full costume today?

ALVA: Of course. Won't you come, too? I must be on stage in five minutes. (*To* LULU.) Unfortunately for me!

GOLL: You know, I've quite forgotten — what's the name of your ballet?

ALVA: *The Dalai Lama.*

GOLL: I thought he was in the asylum.

SCHOEN: No, no, Doctor, you're thinking of Nietzsche.

GOLL: Oh, yes, of course. I always confuse those two.

ALVA: I've helped put Buddhism on its legs.

GOLL: It's by his legs a playwright is known.

ALVA: Corticelli dances the young Buddha as though she'd seen the Light of the World on the Ganges.

SCHOEN: While her mother was still alive, she danced with her feet. . .

ALVA: Then when she was free, she danced with her intelligence. . .

GOLL: But now she dances with her heart!

ALVA: Would you like to see her?

GOLL: Thank you, no.

ALVA: Come with us!

GOLL: I couldn't possibly!

SCHOEN: We really have no time to lose.

ALVA: Come along, Doctor. In the third act you'll see the Dalai Lama in the monastery with his monks. . .

GOLL: I'm only interested in the young Buddha.

ALVA: What's keeping you then?

GOLL: I can't. I simply can't.

ALVA: We're going to Peter's afterwards. There you can express your amazement all you like.

GOLL: You mustn't urge me on so. You really mustn't.

ALVA: You'll see the tame monkeys, the two Brahmins, the little girls. . .

GOLL: In the name of God, will you keep your little girls to yourself!

LULU: Would you reserve a proscenium box for us on Monday, Mr. Alva?

ALVA: How could you doubt it, Madam!

GOLL: When I come back, I'm sure this devil of a Breughel will have completely spoiled my picture for me!

ALVA: That wouldn't be so terrible. It could be painted over easily enough.

GOLL: Unless every brush stroke is explained to our Caravaggio here...

SCHOEN: I think your fears are quite unfounded, Doctor.

GOLL: Next time, gentlemen.

ALVA: My Brahmins are growing impatient. The Daughters of Nirvana are shivering in their tights.

GOLL: Ah, what a blotted mess!

SCHOEN: They'll scold us if we don't bring you along.

GOLL: I'll go back in five minutes. (*He stands downstage left, behind* SCHWARZ, *and compares the picture with* LULU.)

ALVA (*to* LULU): Unfortunately, duty calls me, Madam!

GOLL (*to* SCHWARZ): You should model it a bit more here. The hair is bad. You're not sufficiently interested in your work...

ALVA: Come along.

GOLL: Well, let's go, hip-hop! But ten horses couldn't drag me off to Peter's!

SCHOEN (*following* ALVA *and* GOLL): We'll take my carriage. It's downstairs.

(*They go off.*)

SCHWARZ (*leans to the right and spits out*): Dirty scum! I wish I were dead! — My feed-bag! — Feed-bag and muzzle at the same time! My pride as an artist balks at it! (*After a glance at* LULU.) Pack of fools! (*Rises, goes upstage right, observes* LULU *from all sides, and sits down again at the easel.*) It would be a difficult choice to make. —— Would Madame raise her right hand just a bit higher?

LULU (*grasps the shepherd's crook as high up as possible; to herself*): Who'd have ever thought it possible!

SCHWARZ: I suppose you think I'm ridiculous.

LULU: He'll be right back.

SCHWARZ: All I can do is paint.

LULU: There he is!

SCHWARZ (*rising*): Well?

LULU: Don't you hear?

SCHWARZ: Someone's coming...

LULU: I told you so.

SCHWARZ: It's the caretaker. He's sweeping the stairs.

LULU: Thank God.

SCHWARZ: I suppose you accompany the Doctor on his rounds?

LULU: That's all I need!

SCHWARZ: Because you're not used to being alone.

LULU: We have a housekeeper at home.

SCHWARZ: And she keeps you company?

LULU: She has excellent taste.

SCHWARZ: In what?

LULU: She dresses me.

SCHWARZ: I suppose you go to a great many balls.

LULU: Never.

SCHWARZ: Then why so many clothes?

LULU: For dancing.

SCHWARZ: Do you really dance?

LULU: Czardas — Samaqueca — skirt-dance...

SCHWARZ: Doesn't it disgust you?

LULU: Do you think I'm ugly?

SCHWARZ: You don't quite understand. — Who instructs you?

LULU: He does.

SCHWARZ: Who?

LULU: Him.

SCHWARZ: Him?

LULU: He plays the violin.

SCHWARZ: We learn something new every day.

LULU: I learned in Paris. I took lessons from Eugénie Fougère. She even let me copy her costumes.

SCHWARZ: What are they like?

LULU: There's one with a green lace skirt down to the knees, all with ruffles and décolleté, very décolleté and terribly tight-laced. Then there's a pale green petticoat, and others that keep getting lighter on top of it. And snow-white pantaloons with a hand's-breadth of lace at the bottoms. . .

SCHWARZ: I can't bear anymore. . .

LULU: Then paint!

SCHWARZ (*scraping with his palette-knife*): Aren't you cold?

LULU: Heaven forbid! No. Whatever made you ask that? Are you cold?

SCHWARZ: No. Not today.

LULU: At least I can breathe!

SCHWARZ: I don't understand. . .

(LULU *breathes deeply.*)

SCHWARZ: Would you please not do that! — (*Jumps up, tosses his brush and palette aside, and paces back and forth.*) All the bootblack has to worry about is your feet. And his materials don't devour his money either. If I happen to have no supper tomorrow evening, there won't be any lady of fashion asking me if I know how to swallow oysters.

LULU: What an absolute monster!

SCHWARZ (*takes up his work again*): Why did he have to go to that rehearsal!

LULU: I'd just as soon he'd stayed too.

SCHWARZ: We are really martyrs to our profession.

LULU: I didn't mean to hurt you.

SCHWARZ (*hesitantly, to* LULU): The left leg — would you — just a bit higher. . . ?

LULU: Like this?

SCHWARZ (*goes to the podium*): If you'll allow me. . .

LULU: What do you want?

SCHWARZ: I'll show you.

LULU: You mustn't.

SCHWARZ: You're nervous. (*He tries to take her by the hand.*)

LULU (*throws the shepherd's crook in his face*): Leave me alone! (*She rushes to the main entrance.*) You won't have me for a long time yet.

SCHWARZ: Can't you take a joke?

LULU: Certainly. Just leave me alone. You'll get nowhere with me by force. Get back to your work. You have no right to molest me. (*She runs behind the ottoman.*) Sit down at your easel.

SCHWARZ (*trying to get around the ottoman*): As soon as I've punished you for your capriciousness.

LULU (*evasively*): You'll have to catch me first for that. Go on, you'll never get me. — With a long dress on I'd have fallen into your clutches long ago. — But not as Pierrot!

SCHWARZ (*throwing himself upon the ottoman*): I've got you!

LULU (*throws the tiger-skin over his head*): Good night! (*Jumps across the podium and clambers up the step-ladder.*) I see all the cities of the earth. . .

SCHWARZ (*unwinding himself from the rug*): The little brat!

LULU: I reach up to the heavens and pull down stars for my hair!

SCHWARZ (*climbing after her*): I'll shake till you fall down.

LULU (*climbing higher*): If you don't leave me alone, I'll knock over the ladder. Let go of my legs! — God save Poland!

(*She causes the ladder to topple, jumps onto the podium and, as* SCHWARZ *picks himself from the floor, throws the Spanish screen at him. She rushes downstairs towards the easels.*)

I told you you'd never get me.

SCHWARZ (*coming forward*): I call truce. (*He tries to grab her.*)

LULU: Stay away from me, or. . . (*She throws the easel with the portrait at him, so that both fall crashing to the floor.*)

SCHWARZ (*cries out*): Merciful Heaven!

LULU (*upstage left*): You put that hole in it yourself.

SCHWARZ: I'm ruined! Ten weeks' work! My trip! My exhibition! — There's nothing more to lose! (*He rushes after her.*)

Lulu (*jumps across the ottoman, across the toppled step-ladder, and walks across the podium downstage*): There's a ditch! — Don't fall in! (*Stomps on the portrait.*) So, she made a new man of him, did she? ! (*Falls forward.*)

Schwarz (*stumbling over the Spanish screen*): There will be no mercy now.

Lulu (*upstage*): Leave me alone. — I'm going to faint — O God, O God! (*Comes forward and sinks onto the ottoman.*)

(SCHWARZ *locks the door. Then he sits down beside her, takes her hand and covers it with kisses, then stops suddenly; it is obvious he is fighting an inner battle.*)

Lulu (*opens her eyes*): He might come back.

Schwarz: How do you feel?

Lulu: As if I'd fallen in the water...

Schwarz: I love you.

Lulu: I loved a student once.

Schwarz: Nelly...

Lulu: He had twenty-four dueling scars...

Schwarz: I love you, Nelly.

Lulu: My name is not Nelly.

(SCHWARZ *kisses her.*)

Lulu: My name is Lulu.

Schwarz: I shall call you Eve.

Lulu: Do you know what time it is?

Schwarz (*looking at the clock*): Half-past ten.

(LULU *takes the clock and opens the case.*)

Schwarz: You don't love me.

Lulu: Oh, but I do... It's a few minutes after half-past ten.

SCHWARZ: Kiss me, Eve!

LULU (*takes him by the chin and kisses him; throws the clock in the air and catches it*): You smell of tobacco.

SCHWARZ: Why don't you call me by my first name?

LULU: I'd feel uncomfortable.

SCHWARZ: You're being a hypocrite.

LULU: It seems to me *you're* the hypocrite. — I? Hypocritical? Whatever made you say that? — I *never* needed that.

SCHWARZ (*rises, beside himself, brushing his hand across his brow*): God Almighty! Am I so ignorant of the world — ?

LULU (*screams*): Don't kill me!

SCHWARZ (*turns around quickly*): *You've never loved. . . !*

LULU (*half rising*): *You've never loved. . . !*

GOLL (*outside*): Open this door!

LULU (*has jumped up*): Hide me! O God, please hide me!

GOLL (*pounding at the door*): Open this door!

(SCHWARZ is about to go to the door.)

LULU (*holds him back*): He'll kill me!

GOLL (*pounding at the door*): Open this door!

LULU (*has sunk down in front of* SCHWARZ, *clasping his knees*): He'll kill me! He'll kill me!

SCHWARZ: Stand up. . .

(*The door falls with a crash into the room.*)

(GOLL, *with bloodshot eyes and raised stick, rushes at* SCHWARZ *and* LULU.)

GOLL: You dogs! — You. . . (*He gasps, struggles a second or two for breath, and falls forward onto the floor.*)

(SCHWARZ'*s knees shake.* LULU *has run to the door. — Pause.*)

SCHWARZ (*goes to* GOLL): Sir — Mister — Doctor — Doctor Goll —

LULU (*at the door*): Will you kindly straighten your studio first.

SCHWARZ: Doctor Goll. (*Bends down.*) Doctor. . . (*Steps back.*) He hit his forehead. Help me get him onto the ottoman.

LULU (*pulls back with a shudder*): No, no. . .

SCHWARZ (*tries to turn him over*): Doctor Goll.

LULU: He can't hear you.

SCHWARZ: Will you please help me!

LULU: Not even the two of us can lift him.

SCHWARZ (*straightens up*): We'll have to send for a doctor.

LULU: He's terribly heavy.

SCHWARZ (*taking his hat*): Would you be so kind as to straighten the place a bit while I'm gone? (*He goes off.*)

LULU: Oh, he's suddenly going to jump up. — (*Intensely.*) Bussi! —— He doesn't notice a thing.— (*Comes forward in a wide arc.*) He's looking at my feet — he's watching every step I take. He won't take his eyes off me. (*She touches him with the toe of her shoe.*) Bussi! — (*Recoiling.*) He's serious. —— The party's over. —— He's walking out on me. —— What shall I do? —— (*Bends down to the ground.*) What a strange, wild face! — (*Straightening up.*) And no one here to give him the last rites. — How very sad. . .

SCHWARZ (*entering*): Still unconscious?

LULU (*downstage left*): What shall I do. . .

SCHWARZ (*bent over* GOLL): Doctor Goll.

LULU: I almost think he's serious.

SCHWARZ: You might be a bit more dignified about it.

LULU: He would never have spoken to me that way. He would ask me to dance for him when he didn't feel well.

SCHWARZ: The doctor should be here any second.

LULU: No doctor can help him now.

SCHWARZ: In a case like this you do whatever you can.

LULU: He doesn't believe in it himself.

SCHWARZ: Don't you at least want to change?

LULU: Yes. — In a moment.

SCHWARZ: What are you waiting for?

LULU: Please. . .

SCHWARZ: What. . . ?

LULU: Close his eyes.

SCHWARZ: You're horrible.

LULU: Not nearly as horrible as you.

SCHWARZ: I?

LULU: You're a natural born criminal.

SCHWARZ: Doesn't this move you at all?

LULU: It'll happen to me too someday.

SCHWARZ: That was uncalled for at a time like this.

LULU: Please. . .

SCHWARZ: Do whatever you think necessary. I know nothing about such matters.

LULU (*to the right of* GOLL): He's looking at me.

SCHWARZ (*to the left of* GOLL): At me too. . .

LULU: You're a coward.

SCHWARZ (*closes* GOLL'*s eyes with a handkerchief*): This is the first time in my life I've had to do such a thing.

LULU: You didn't do it for your mother?

SCHWARZ (*nervously*): No.

LULU: Were you away from home?

SCHWARZ: No!

LULU: Or were you afraid?

SCHWARZ (*violently*): No.

LULU (*starts back*): I didn't mean to insult you.

SCHWARZ: She's still alive.

LULU: Then you still have someone.

SCHWARZ: She's poor as a beggar.

LULU: I know what that means.

SCHWARZ: Don't mock me.

LULU: But now I'm rich. . .

SCHWARZ: It makes my flesh creep. (*He goes left.*) It's not her fault!

LULU (*to herself*): What shall I do now?

SCHWARZ (*to himself*): She's totally depraved!

(*SCHWARZ at left, LULU at right, look across mistrustfully at each other.—SCHWARZ goes to her and takes her hand.*)

SCHWARZ: Look me in the eyes!

LULU (*fearfully*): What do you want?

SCHWARZ (*leads her to the ottoman and makes her sit beside him*): Look me in the eyes!

LULU: I see my reflection as Pierrot.

SCHWARZ (*pushes her from him*): Damn your dancing!

LULU: I have to change. . .

SCHWARZ (*holds her back*): Just one question. . .

LULU: I can't answer you.

SCHWARZ (*at the ottoman again*): Can you tell the truth?

LULU: I don't know.

SCHWARZ: Do you believe in a Creator?

LULU: I don't know.

SCHWARZ: Is there anything you can swear by?

LULU: I don't know. Leave me alone! You've lost your mind!

SCHWARZ: What *do* you believe in?

LULU: I don't know.

SCHWARZ: Do you have a soul?

LULU: I don't know.

SCHWARZ: Have you ever been in love?

LULU: I don't know.

SCHWARZ (*rises, walks to the left; to himself*): She doesn't know!

LULU (*without moving*): I don't know.

SCHWARZ (*with a glance at* GOLL): But *he* knows. . .

LULU (*going to him*): What do you want to know?

SCHWARZ (*indignantly*): Go and get dressed!

(LULU *goes off into the bedroom.*)

SCHWARZ: Oh, God, how I wish I could change places with you! — I'll give her back to you. I'll even give you my youth. I have neither courage nor faith. I've had to be patient too long. And now it's too late. I'm not prepared for happiness. It terrifies me. Wake up! I haven't touched her. He's opening his mouth. — Mouth wide and eyes closed, just like a child. It's the other way around with me. Wake up! Wake up! (*Kneels down and ties a handkerchief around* GOLL'*s head.*) I pray that heaven will let me be happy — that it give me the strength and the freedom of soul to be just slightly happy. For her sake — only for her sake.

(LULU *enters fully dressed from the bedroom, her hat on, and her right hand under her left arm.*)

LULU (*to* SCHWARZ, *raising her left arm*): Would you hook me up back here? My hand is shaking.

ACT TWO

A very elegant salon. The main entrance, upstage right. Downstage right and left, portieres. A number of steps lead to the one on the left. Situated on the rear wall is the picture of LULU *as Pierrot, in a magnificent brocade frame. A tall mirror to the left. In front of it a chaise longue. To the right, a writing desk of ebony. In the center, several armchairs are placed around a small Chinese table.*

LULU, *dressed in a green silk morning-gown, stands motionless in front of the mirror, furrows her brow, runs her hand across it, touches her cheeks, moves from the mirror with a discontented, half angry look. She goes to the right, turning several times, opens a box on the writing desk, lights a cigarette, then looks through the books lying on the table. She picks one up, lies down on the chaise longue opposite the mirror. Then, after a moment of reading, lets the book fall, nods seriously to herself, and once again takes up the book.* SCHWARZ, *with brush and palette in hand, enters from the right, bends over* LULU, *kisses her on the forehead, goes up the steps at the left, and turns around at the portiere.*

SCHWARZ: Eve!

LULU (*smiling*): Yes?

SCHWARZ: I think you look exceptionally charming today.

LULU (*with a glance at the mirror*): That depends on what you expect.

SCHWARZ: Your hair smells fresh as morning. . .

LULU: I just came from my bath.

SCHWARZ (*approaching her*): I have a lot to do today.

LULU: You just think you have.

SCHWARZ (*puts his brush and palette on the rug and sits on the edge of the chaise longue*): What are you reading?

LULU (*reading*): "She suddenly heard an anchor of refuge come nodding up the stairs."

SCHWARZ: Who in the world writes so touchingly?

LULU (*reading*): "The postman with a money-order."

(HENRIETTE *enters through the main entrance, a hatbox under her arm. She places a salver with letters on the table.*)

HENRIETTE: The mail. — I'm taking the hat to the milliner's now. Has Madame any further orders?

LULU: No.

(SCHWARZ *motions for her to leave.* HENRIETTE *goes off with a cunning smile.*)

SCHWARZ: What did you dream about last night?

LULU: You've asked me that twice today already.

SCHWARZ (*rises, takes the letters from the salver*): News makes me absolutely tremble. I'm afraid everyday that the world is simply going to collapse. (*Goes back to the chaise longue and hands* LULU *a letter.*) For you.

LULU (*smells the envelope*): It's from Corticelli. (*Drops it into her bosom.*)

SCHWARZ (*rushing through a letter*): My Samaqueca dancer was sold — for fifty-thousand Marks!

LULU: Who wrote you that?

SCHWARZ: Sedelmeier in Paris. That's the third picture since our marriage. I scarcely know what to do with so much good fortune.

LULU (*pointing to the letters*): And there are more.

SCHWARZ (*opening an engagement announcement*): Look at this! (*He gives it to* LULU.)

LULU (*reading*): "Heinrich Ritter von Zornikow has the honor of announcing the engagement of his daughter Charlotte Marie Adelaide to Doctor Ludwig Schoen."

SCHWARZ (*opening another letter*): Well, at last! It's taken him an eternity to make a public announcement. I can't understand that of so despotic a man, and with all his influence. What could possibly be preventing his marriage?

LULU: What's that you're reading?

SCHWARZ: An invitation to participate in the International Exhibition in St. Petersburg. — I haven't the faintest idea what to paint.

LULU: Some charming little girl or other, of course.

SCHWARZ: Would you care to pose for it?

LULU: I dare say there are enough other pretty girls around.

SCHWARZ: Other models don't seem to make full use of my capacities — no matter *how* suggestive they may be.

LULU: Then I suppose I'll have to. — Couldn't we just as well do one lying down?

SCHWARZ: I'd really prefer leaving the pose to you. (*Folding the letters.*) Let's don't forget to send Schoen our congratulations today. (*He goes to the right and puts the letters in the writing desk.*)

LULU: We did that a long time ago.

SCHWARZ: Then for the bride's sake.

LULU: Write him if you like.

SCHWARZ: And now to work. (*He picks up his brush and palette, kisses* LULU, *goes towards the steps at the left, and turns in the portiere.*) Eve!

LULU (*lets her book sink down, smiling*): Yes?

SCHWARZ (*going to her*): It seems that every day I see you, it's always for the very first time.

LULU: Oh, you're horrible.

SCHWARZ (*sinks to his knees beside the chaise longue and fondles her hand*): And it's all your fault.

LULU (*stroking his hair*): You're wasting me.

SCHWARZ: But you belong to me. And God knows, you're never more fascinating than when by all rights you should be ugly for an hour or two. Since I've had you, I've had nothing else. — I've become completely lost to myself. . .

LULU: Don't get so excited.

(*A bell rings in the hallway.*)

SCHWARZ (*starts*): Damn!

LULU: There's no one at home!

SCHWARZ: It might be the picture dealer. . .

LULU: I don't care if it's the Emperor of China.

SCHWARZ: Just a moment. (*He goes off.*)

LULU (*as though seeing a vision*): You? — You? — (*She closes her eyes.*)

SCHWARZ (*reenters*): A beggar who says he was in the war. (*Picks up his brush and palette.*) And it's about time I settled down to work too. (*Goes off left.*)

(LULU *tidies herself in front of the mirror, smooths back her hair, and goes out.*)

(SCHIGOLCH *enters, led in by* LULU.)

SCHIGOLCH: I'd imagined him to be a bit more chivalrous,

somewhat more authority. He was rather awkward. His knees seemed to giveway when he saw me.

LULU (*pushes up a chair for him*): How could you possibly beg from him?

SCHIGOLCH: That's exactly what I dragged my seventy-seven summers here to do. You told me he spent all his mornings painting.

LULU: He wasn't quite awake yet. How much do you need?

SCHIGOLCH: Two hundred, if you have that much in cash; or, for that matter, three hundred. Some clients of mine have vanished into thin air.

LULU (*goes to the writing desk and rummages about in it*): I'm so tired.

SCHIGOLCH (*looking around*): That's another thing that brought me here. I've wanted so long to see what your house looked like.

LULU: And?

SCHIGOLCH: Overwhelming. (*Looking upwards.*) Like my *own* house fifty years ago. Instead of these hangings we had rusty swords. My God, you've certainly got on in the world. (*Shuffling his feet.*) The carpets . . .

LULU (*gives him two bills*): I prefer to walk on them barefoot.

SCHIGOLCH (*looking at* LULU's *portrait*): Is that you?

LULU (*winking*): Isn't it lovely?

SCHIGOLCH: Even if it were only the best possible.

LULU: Would you like something sweet?

SCHIGOLCH: Such as?

LULU (*rises*): Elixir de Spa.

SCHIGOLCH: That won't help me. — Does *he* drink?

LULU (*takes out a decanter and some glasses from the cabinet near the fireplace*): Not yet. (*Coming downstage.*) The cordial has different effects on different people.

SCHIGOLCH: Does he go wild?

LULU (*filling two glasses*): He goes to sleep.

SCHIGOLCH: When he's drunk you can see straight through to his insides.

LULU: I'd prefer not to. (*She sits opposite* SCHIGOLCH.) Tell me about yourself.

SCHIGOLCH: Streets grow longer and my legs shorter.

LULU: And your harmonica?

SCHIGOLCH: Broken-winded — like me with my asthma. I keep thinking it's not worth trying to improve. (*He clinks glasses with her.*)

LULU (*empties the glass*): I thought you'd run your rope a long time ago. . .

SCHIGOLCH: So did I. But you're not allowed to rest even after sunset. I'm hoping winter will help me. I expect then my — (*He coughs.*) — asthma will help me find a way out.

LULU (*filling the glasses*): Do you think they've forgotten you over there?

SCHIGOLCH: Possibly. It's certainly going according to the rules. (*Stroking her knee.*) Now you tell me about yourself. — It's been a long time — my dear little Lulu.

LULU (*pulling back; smiling*): Life is quite incomprehensible.

SCHIGOLCH: What could you know about such things! You're still so young.

LULU: Imagine you calling me Lulu.

SCHIGOLCH: You mean it's not "Lulu"? I've never called you anything else.

LULU: I haven't been called "Lulu" as long as I can remember.

SCHIGOLCH: Then *what?*

LULU: "Lulu" sounds so old-fashioned.

SCHIGOLCH: Heaven help us!

LULU: They call me. . .

SCHIGOLCH: As if the principle weren't always the same. . . !

LULU: I don't understand.

SCHIGOLCH: What *do* they call you?

LULU: Eve.

SCHIGOLCH: Six of one, half dozen of the other.

LULU: Well, that's what I answer to.

SCHIGOLCH (*looks around*): I always dreamed you'd have something like this. You were made for it. What's that supposed to be?

LULU (*spraying herself with a bottle of perfume*): Heliotrope.

SCHIGOLCH: Does it smell any better than you?

LULU (*spraying him*): That needn't bother you any longer.

SCHIGOLCH: Who'd have imagined such luxury!

LULU: When I think back — ugh!

SCHIGOLCH (*stroking her knee*): How have you been? Are you still studying French?

LULU: I sleep most of the time.

SCHIGOLCH: Very genteel. That always looks good. And?

LULU: I stretch — till my bones crack.

SCHIGOLCH: And when they've finished cracking?

LULU: Why should that interest you?

SCHIGOLCH: Why should it interest me? Why should it interest me? I'd rather live till Doomsday and renounce all Heavenly bliss than leave my little Lulu behind here, penniless. Why should that interest me? I sympathize with you. My better self has already been transfigured. But I'm still deeply sensitive to the things of this world.

LULU: I'm not.

SCHIGOLCH: You're too well off.

LULU (*shuddering*): That's ridiculous...

SCHIGOLCH: You're better off than with your dancing-bear.

LULU (*sadly*): I don't dance anymore...

SCHIGOLCH: High time for him to stop, too.

LULU: Now I'm... (*She stops short.*)

SCHIGOLCH: Tell me what you really feel, child. I had faith in you when all I could see were your two big eyes. What are you now?

LULU: An animal...

SCHIGOLCH: The devil you are! — Ah, but what an animal! A delicate animal! An elegant animal! — A magnificent animal! —— Yes, they can bury me now. — We're through with prejudices. Even against the woman who'll lay me out and wash my corpse.

LULU: You needn't worry about being washed.

SCHIGOLCH: It doesn't matter. We get dirty afterwards anyway.

LULU (*spraying him*): It would bring you back to life.

SCHIGOLCH: We're nothing but dust.

LULU: I beg your pardon! I rub myself with oil, and powder everyday.

SCHIGOLCH: Probably worth it, too, for that coxcomb's sake.

LULU: It makes my skin feel like satin.

SCHIGOLCH: As though it were still anything less than dirt.

LULU: Thank you. But I'd like to be good enough to eat.

SCHIGOLCH: Oh, all of us are that. At some future time there'll be a great dinner down below. It'll be open house.

LULU: Whoever feeds off you won't have much to worry about.

SCHIGOLCH: Patience, child. Your admirers won't put you in alcohol either. It's "fair Melusine" as long as there's any go still left in her. And afterwards? They wouldn't even have her in the zoo. (*Rising.*) She'd give the precious beasties stomach cramps.

LULU (*rising*): Have you had enough?

SCHIGOLCH: There'll be enough left over to plant a terebinth tree on my grave. — I'll find my own way out. (*He goes off.*)

(LULU *accompanies him out and returns with* DOCTOR SCHOEN.)

SCHOEN: What was your father doing here?

LULU: What's the matter with you?

SCHOEN: If I were your husband, that man would never set foot in my house.

LULU: You may call me Lulu if you like. He's not here.

SCHOEN: The honor is mine.

LULU: I don't understand.

SCHOEN: I know. (*Offering her a chair.*) That's precisely what I want to talk to you about.

LULU (*sitting down uncertainly*): Why didn't you tell me yesterday?

SCHOEN: I'd rather you don't mention yesterday. I told you that two years ago.

LULU (*nervously*): I see. Hm.

SCHOEN: I wish you'd stop coming to my house.

LULU: Would you like an Elixir...

SCHOEN: Thank you, no. Do you understand?

(LULU *shakes her head.*)

SCHOEN: Very well. The choice is yours.—You're forcing me into extreme measures.—You will either act in accordance with your position...

LULU: Or?

SCHOEN: Or—you will force me to—I shall have to go straight to that person responsible for your behavior.

LULU: How do you propose to do that.

SCHOEN: I'll request your husband to supervise all your activities.

(LULU *rises and goes up the steps at the left.*)

SCHOEN: Where are you going?

LULU (*calls through the curtains*): Walter!

SCHOEN (*jumping up*): You've lost your mind!

LULU (*turning back*): Aha!

SCHOEN: I'm making superhuman efforts to raise you in society. You can be ten times prouder of your name than of your intimacy with me...

LULU (*comes down the steps, puts her arms around* SCHOEN'S *neck*): Why are you still afraid? You have everything you want.

SCHOEN: This is not a joke. Everything I want? I've finally

become engaged. I now hope to bring my bride into a respectable home.

LULU (*sitting down*): She's become a real enchantress these last two years.

SCHOEN: She doesn't see through people as earnestly as before.

LULU: Then she's just now become a real woman. We can meet each other wherever you think proper.

SCHOEN: We will meet each other nowhere but in the presence of your husband.

LULU: I don't think you believe what you're saying.

SCHOEN: The important thing is that *he* believes it. Go on, call him. His marriage to you and all I've done for him have made him my friend.

LULU (*rising*): Mine too.

SCHOEN: Then I'll cut down the sword hanging over my head.

LULU: The fact is you've put me in chains. And yet I owe you my happiness. You'll make friends by the score, once you have a pretty young wife again.

SCHOEN: You judge other women according to yourself.—He's like a child. Otherwise he'd have discovered your infidelities long ago.

LULU: I only wish he had! For then he could put away his swaddling-clothes. He trusts in the fact he carries his marriage contract in his pocket. Whatever trouble and effort there was is past now. One can give and let himself go as if in his own home. He's not childish. He's banal. He has no education. He sees nothing. He sees neither me nor himself. He's blind, blind, blind. . .

SCHOEN (*half to himself*): Wait till his eyes are opened.

LULU: Why don't you open them for him? I'm going to pieces. I'm neglecting myself. I don't recognize me any-more. What am I to him? He calls me his sweet little devil. He'd say the same to any old-maid piano teacher. He makes no pretensions. Everything is just fine with him. That's because he's never once in his life felt the need for a woman.

SCHOEN: Is that true?

LULU: He admits it.

SCHOEN: A man who's painted every kind of woman imaginable since he was fourteen?

LULU: He's afraid of women. He worries about his health.—But he's not afraid of *me!*

SCHOEN: God knows how happy other girls would be in your shoes.

LULU (*pleading tenderly*): Lead him astray. You know how if anyone. Put him in bad company. You know the people. I'm nothing more nor less to him than a woman, just a woman. He makes me feel like a fool. Perhaps it will make him prouder of me. Right now he doesn't know the difference. All I do is try to find ways to shake him up. I dance the can-can in despair. He yawns and drivels something about obscenity.

SCHOEN: That's ridiculous. He's an artist.

LULU: At least he thinks he is.

SCHOEN: Which is the main thing after all.

LULU: When I pose for him. He also thinks he's a famous man.

SCHOEN: And he *is*. We've *made* him one.

LULU: He believes everything. He's as mistrustful as a thief, but lets himself be lied to until you lose all respect for him. When we were getting to know each other, I told him I had never loved. . .

(SCHOEN *falls into an armchair.*)

LULU: Otherwise he'd have taken me for a fallen woman.

SCHOEN: —God knows the exorbitant demands you make on legitimate relationships!

LULU: I *don't* make exorbitant demands. I often still have dreams of Goll.

SCHOEN: At least he wasn't banal.

LULU: It's as though he had never left. That's how much he's here. Except he tiptoes about in stocking feet. He isn't angry with me. He's terribly sad. And afraid of being here without police permission. One thing he can't get over is that I've thrown away so much money since. . .

SCHOEN: What you miss is the whip.

LULU: Perhaps. I don't dance anymore.

SCHOEN: You must teach him how.

LULU: It wouldn't be worth the trouble!

SCHOEN: Ninety out of every hundred women educate their husbands to suit themselves.

LULU: He loves me.

SCHOEN: That's an unbridgeable abyss.

LULU: He doesn't know the first thing about me, but he loves me. If he had so much as the faintest idea of me, he'd tie a stone around my neck and throw me into the deepest part of the ocean.

SCHOEN (*rising*): Let's put an end to this!

LULU: Whatever you say.

SCHOEN: I married you off. I married you off twice. You live in luxury. I created a position for your husband. If that doesn't satisfy you, and he laughs up his sleeve, well, I'm not making any idealistic demands, but — just leave me out of it.

LULU (*with determination*): If I belong to anyone in the world, I belong to you. Without you I — I don't know where I'd be. You took me by the hand, you fed me, clothed me — and just as I was about to steal your watch. Do you think I can forget that? Anyone else would have called the police. You sent me to school and taught me manners. Except for you, no one in the whole world has ever given me a second thought. I danced, I posed, and I was happy earning my living that way. But I can't love by command.

SCHOEN (*raising his voice*): Leave me out of it. Do whatever you want. I didn't come here to cause a scandal. I came to get rid of one. My connections with you have caused me sacrifice enough. I assumed that with a healthy young man, such as no woman your age could equal, you would finally be satisfied. If you feel indebted to me, then please don't throw yourself at me a third time. Must I wait even longer to secure my share? Must I risk having my successful concessions fail after two years? What good does your being married do me, when you can be seen coming and going from my house at any hour of the day or night?—Why the hell couldn't Doctor Goll have lived just one more year? You were in excellent safekeeping with him. By that time I'd have had my new home established.

LULU: And then what would you have had? The child gets on your nerves. The child is too innocent for you. The child was far too carefully raised. What objection could I have to your marriage? But you've deceived yourself if you think just because of your impending marriage you can express your contempt of me.

SCHOEN: Contempt? ! — I shall shape that child precisely as I want her! If anything is contemptible, it's your intrigues!

LULU (*laughing*): Do you really think me jealous of the child? — I'd never have thought of that...

SCHOEN: Why do you call her "the child"? That "child" is scarcely a year younger than you. Allow me the freedom to live what life I still have left. However the child was brought up, she has five senses just as you have...

(SCHWARZ *enters through the left portiere, his brush in hand.*)

SCHWARZ: What's the matter?

LULU (*to* SCHOEN): Well, say something.

SCHWARZ: What's the matter with you two?

LULU: Nothing that concerns you...

SCHOEN (*quickly*): Be quiet!

LULU: He's had enough of me.

(SCHWARZ *leads* LULU *off left.* — SCHOEN *pages through one of the books on the table.*)

SCHOEN: It had to come out sometime. —— I have to get out of this!

SCHWARZ (*returns*): Is this supposed to be a joke?

SCHOEN (*indicating an armchair*): Would you please sit down.

SCHWARZ: What is it?

SCHOEN: Sit down.

SCHWARZ (*sits down*): Well?

SCHOEN (*sits down*): You've married half a million. . .

SCHWARZ: Is it gone?

SCHOEN: Not a cent of it.

SCHWARZ: Would you mind explaining all this?

SCHOEN: You've married half a million. . .

SCHWARZ: Is that a crime?

SCHOEN: You've made a name for yourself. You're free to work without disturbance. You needn't deny yourself anything. . .

SCHWARZ: What do you have against me?

SCHOEN: For six months now you've lived in absolute bliss. You have a wife whose merits the world envies you, and who deserves a husband she can respect. . .

SCHWARZ: You mean she doesn't respect me?

SCHOEN: No.

SCHWARZ (*uneasily*): — I came from the dark depths of society. She came from up there. I have no greater wish than to be her equal. (*Extending his hand to* SCHOEN.) Thank you.

SCHOEN (*shaking his head, half embarrassed*): Not at all, not at all!

SCHWARZ (*with determination*): Continue!

SCHOEN: Keep her under closer watch.

SCHWARZ: I? On her?

SCHOEN: We're not children. We don't trifle. We live. — She demands to be taken seriously. Her merits are such that she should be given that right.

SCHWARZ: What has she done?

SCHOEN: You've married half a million!

SCHWARZ (*rises, beside himself*): You. . .

SCHOEN (*taking him by the shoulder*): We needn't get angry. (*Forces him to sit down.*) We must speak to each other very seriously.

SCHWARZ: What has she done?

SCHOEN: First consider all the things you have her to thank for, and then. . .

SCHWARZ: What has she done? — Tell me!

SCHOEN: And then take responsibility for your own faults and blame them on no one else.

SCHWARZ: With whom? With whom?

SCHOEN: If you think a duel is called for...

SCHWARZ: When did this start?

SCHOEN (*evasively*): I didn't come here to start a scandal; I came to save you from one.

SCHWARZ (*slapping his head*): You misunderstood her.

SCHOEN (*embarrassed*): That's not enough for me. I can't see you continue living in such blindness. The girl deserves to be a respectable woman. Since I've known her she's changed for the better.

SCHWARZ: Since you've known her? — Since when have you known her?

SCHOEN: Since she was about twelve.

SCHWARZ (*confused*): She's never told me that.

SCHOEN: She was selling flowers outside the Cafe Alhambra. Every night between twelve and two she would push her way barefoot among the guests.

SCHWARZ: She's never told me that.

SCHOEN: And she was right not to. I'm telling you this to show you it's not a question of moral degeneracy. On the contrary, the girl has developed remarkably.

SCHWARZ: She told me she'd grown up with an aunt.

SCHOEN: That was the woman to whom I entrusted her. She was the best pupil. Mothers would always hold her up as an example to their own children. She has a sense of duty. It's no one's mistake but yours if you've failed to bring out the best in her.

SCHWARZ (*sobbing*): My God! ...

SCHOEN (*emphatically*): What do you mean, "my God!"? There's nothing in the world could change the happiness you've experienced. What's done is done! You're overestimating yourself against your better judgment if you think yourself the loser. You *have* to win! But going around crying "my God!" isn't going to do it for you. I've never in my life shown you greater friendship than in this. I'm speaking openly and offering you my help. So don't be unworthy of it.

SCHWARZ (*from this point on goes more and more to pieces*): When I was getting to know her she said she'd never yet been in love.

SCHOEN: Imagine a widow saying such a thing. It's to her credit she chose you for a husband. Make the same demands upon yourself and your happiness is unstained.

SCHWARZ: They say he made her wear short dresses.

SCHOEN: But he married her! — That was a master stroke on her part. I'll never understand how she brought him to that state. You must know the answer to that yourself. You're enjoying the fruits of her diplomacy.

SCHWARZ: How did Doctor Goll get to know her?

SCHOEN: Through me. — It was after the death of my first wife, and as I was making overtures to my present fiancee. She came between us. She'd decided to become my wife.

SCHWARZ (*as though seized with a horrible suspicion*): And when her husband died?

SCHOEN: You've married half a million! !

SCHWARZ (*wailing*): I wish I'd stayed where I was! I wish I'd died of hunger!

SCHOEN (*with a superior tone*): Do you suppose *I'm* making no concession myself? Who doesn't make concessions? You've married half a million. You're one of the biggest painters of the day. You don't get there without money. You're not the person to sit in judgment on her. The standards of bourgeois society simply don't apply to a background such as Mignon has had.

SCHWARZ (*quite bewildered*): Who are you talking about?

SCHOEN: I'm talking about her father. As I said, you're an artist. Your ideals exist in quite a different realm from those of a common day-laborer.

SCHWARZ: I don't understand you.

SCHOEN: I'm talking about the inhuman conditions from which this girl has developed herself — thanks to her upbringing!

SCHWARZ: But who?

SCHOEN: Who? — Your wife!

SCHWARZ: Eve??

SCHOEN: I called her Mignon.

SCHWARZ: I thought her name was Nelly.

SCHOEN: That's what Doctor Goll called her.

SCHWARZ: And I called her Eve. . .

SCHOEN: What her real name was, I'm afraid I don't know.

SCHWARZ (*absently*): Perhaps *she* knows.

SCHOEN: With a father like hers she's a miracle, even with all her failings. I don't understand you. . .

SCHWARZ: Did he die in an asylum. . . ?

SCHOEN: He was just here.

SCHWARZ: Who was just here?

SCHOEN: Her father.

SCHWARZ: Here? In this house?

SCHOEN: He made himself scarce when I came in. Look, here are the glasses.

SCHWARZ: She told me he'd died in an asylum.

SCHOEN (*encouragingly*): Make her feel you have authority. All she wants is to show absolute obedience. She was divinely happy with Doctor Goll, because there was no joking where he was concerned.

SCHWARZ (*shaking his head*): She said she'd never yet loved. . .

SCHOEN: You must begin with yourself. Now pull yourself together.

SCHWARZ: She swore to me!

SCHOEN: You can demand no sense of duty from her until you know where your own task lies.

SCHWARZ: By her mother's grave! !

SCHOEN: She never knew her mother — not to mention where her grave is. — Her mother doesn't have a grave.

SCHWARZ (*despairingly*): I have no place in society.

SCHOEN: What's wrong with you?

SCHWARZ: A terrible pain. . .

SCHOEN (*rises, steps back; after a pause*): Guard her for yourself — she's yours. — This is a decisive moment. She might well be lost to you tomorrow.

SCHWARZ (*pointing to his chest*): Here—here. . .

SCHOEN: You've married half a—(*Reflecting.*) Let the moment slip and she's lost to you.

SCHWARZ: If only I could cry!—Oh, if only I could scream!

SCHOEN (*puts a hand on his shoulder*): I can see how you're suffering. . .

SCHWARZ (*rising, with apparent calm*): You're right, quite right.

SCHOEN (*grasping his hand*): Where are you going?

SCHWARZ: To talk to her.

SCHOEN: Excellent!

(SCHOEN *walks* SCHWARZ *to the door, right.* SCHWARZ *goes out.* SCHOEN *returns.*)

SCHOEN: That was tough work. (*After a pause; looking left.*) Surely he took her into his studio before—

(*Terrible groans are heard from off right.*)

SCHOEN (*hurries to the door at right; finds it locked*): Open up! Open up!

LULU (*entering through the portiere at left*): What. . . ?

SCHOEN: Open up!

LULU (*comes down the steps*): How horrible.

SCHOEN: Is there an ax in the kitchen?

LULU: He'll open it. . .

SCHOEN: I don't want to break it in.

LULU: When he's finished crying.

SCHOEN (*kicking at the door*): Open up! (*To* LULU.) Get me an ax!

LULU: Get a doctor. . .

SCHOEN: You've lost your mind!

LULU: It serves you right.

(*A bell rings in the hallway.* SCHOEN *slips upstage and stands in the doorway.*)

SCHOEN: I shouldn't be seen here just now.

LULU: It might be the picture-dealer.

(*The bell rings again.*)

SCHOEN: But if we don't answer. . .

(LULU *steals towards the door.*)

SCHOEN (*holds her back*): Stay here. After all, one isn't always readily available. (*He tiptoes out.*)

(LULU *returns to the locked door and listens.*)

(SCHOEN *shows in* ALVA.)

SCHOEN: Please be quiet.

ALVA (*very excitedly*): But a revolution's broken out in Paris.

SCHOEN: Be quiet.

ALVA (*to* LULU): You're white as a ghost.

SCHOEN (*rattling the door*): Walter! — Walter!

(*The sound of a death-rattle is heard.*)

LULU: May God have mercy on you. . .

SCHOEN: Haven't you brought the ax?

LULU: I don't even know if there is one. . . (*She goes off hesitantly, upstage right.*)

ALVA: He's trying to mystify us.

SCHOEN: A revolution in Paris? !

ALVA: They're beating their heads against the wall at the newspaper office. No one knows what to write.

(*A bell rings in the hallway.*)

SCHOEN (*kicking at the door*): Walter!

ALVA: Shall I break it in?

SCHOEN: I can do that myself. Now who can that be! (*Straightening up.*) He has the nerve to enjoy life while he can and let others take the responsibility for it!

LULU (*returns with an ax*): Henriette just got back.

SCHOEN: Close the door.

ALVA: Give it here. (*He takes the ax and brings it down between the doorpost and the lock.*)

SCHOEN: You have to get a firmer grip on it.

ALVA: It's coming.

(*The door flies open.* ALVA *drops the ax and staggers back.* —— *Pause.*)

LULU (*pointing to the door; to* SCHOEN): After you. (SCHOEN *shrinks back.*)

LULU: Are you — dizzy. . . ?

(SCHOEN *wipes the perspiration from his brow and goes in.*)

ALVA (*on the chaise longue*): Horrible!

LULU (*holds to the doorpost, her hand at her mouth, screams sharply*): Oh! — Oh! (*Rushes to* ALVA.) I can't stay here!

ALVA: Ghastly!

LULU (*taking him by the hand*): Come on.

ALVA: But where?

LULU: I can't be alone. (*She goes off left with* ALVA.)

(SCHOEN *returns from stage right, a ring of keys in his hand. There is blood on his hand. He pulls the door shut, goes to the writing table, opens it and writes two notes.*)

ALVA (*entering from the left*): She's changing clothes. . .

SCHOEN: She's gone?

ALVA: To her room. She's changing.

(SCHOEN *rings the bell.* HENRIETTE *enters.*)

SCHOEN: You know where Doctor Bernstein lives.

HENRIETTE: Of course, Doctor. Right next door.

SCHOEN (*giving her a note*): Take this over to him.

HENRIETTE: And if the doctor isn't at home?

SCHOEN: He's at home. (*Giving her the other note.*) And this one to the police station. Take a cab.

(HENRIETTE *runs off.*)

SCHOEN: This is a judgment upon me.

ALVA: My blood feels frozen.

SCHOEN (*to the right*): The fool!

ALVA: He was so wrapped up in himself.

(LULU *appears on the step at the left in a duster and pointed hat.*)

ALVA: Where do you expect to go?

LULU: Out. I see it written on all the walls.

SCHOEN: Where did he keep his papers?

LULU: In the writing table.

SCHOEN (*at the writing table*): Where?

LULU: The bottom right-hand drawer. (*She kneels down in front of the writing table, opens the drawer and empties the papers on the floor.*) Here. There's nothing to be afraid of. He had no secrets.

SCHOEN: I might just as well retire from the world right now.

LULU (*kneeling*): Write an article about him. Call him Michelangelo.

SCHOEN: What good would that do? — (*Points to his right.*) There lies my engagement.

ALVA: The hazards of your game.

SCHOEN: Scream it out in the streets!

ALVA (*pointing at* LULU): If only you'd treated that girl fairly when my mother died!

SCHOEN (*to the right*): My engagement lies in there, bleeding!

LULU (*rising*): I won't stay here any longer.

SCHOEN: In an hour the newsboys will be hawking their Extras. I don't dare go out on the streets.

LULU: What could you do about it?

SCHOEN: That's just it! They'll stone me!

ALVA: You'll have to go away.

SCHOEN: And leave this scandal an open field?

LULU (*at the chaise longue*): He was lying here just ten minutes ago.

SCHOEN: This is the thanks I get for all I did for him! My life's work destroyed in a second!

ALVA: Control yourself, please!

LULU (*on the chaise longue*): We're among friends.

ALVA: And how!

SCHOEN (*to* LULU): What will you tell the police?

LULU: Nothing.

ALVA: He wanted to give back to Fate precisely what she gave him.

LULU: His first thoughts were always of murder.

SCHOEN: He possessed what most people only dream of!

LULU: He paid dearly for it, too.

ALVA: He had something that we don't have!

SCHOEN (*with sudden violence*): I know your reasons! I have no cause to be considerate of you! The very fact that you do everything to avoid having any brothers and sisters is all the more reason for me to bring up other children!

ALVA: You're a bad judge of human nature.

LULU: Why not bring out your own Extra?

SCHOEN (*with violent indignation*): He had no sense of morality! (*In sudden control of himself again.*) A revolution in Paris — ?

ALVA: Our editors act as though they'd been struck by lightning. Everything's come to a standstill.

SCHOEN: That will help me recover from this. —— If only the police would come. Time is more precious now than gold.

(*A bell rings in the hallway.*)

ALVA: There they are. . .

(SCHOEN *is about to go to the door.*)

LULU (*jumps up*): No, wait, there's blood on you.

SCHOEN: Where? . . .

LULU: Wait, I'll wipe it off. (*She sprinkles her handkerchief with perfume and wipes the blood from* SCHOEN'S *hand.*)

SCHOEN: It's your husband's blood.

LULU: It won't stain.

SCHOEN: You're a monster.

LULU: You'll marry me all the same.

(*The bell in the hall rings.*)

LULU: Patience, my dear, patience.

(SCHOEN *goes off upstage right.* — *He returns, leading in* ESCHERICH, *a reporter.*)

ESCHERICH (*out of breath*): Allow me to — to — to introduce myself. . .

SCHOEN: Have you been running?

ESCHERICH (*handing him a card*): From the police station. . . they said it was a suicide. . .

SCHOEN (*reading*): Fritz Escherich, correspondent of *The* —. Come this way, please.

ESCHERICH: Just a moment. (*Takes out his notebook and a pencil, writes a few words, bows to* LULU, *writes, turns towards the broken door, writes.*) An ax. . . (*Is about to lift it.*)

SCHOEN (*restraining him*): Please don't touch it.

ESCHERICH (*writes*): Door broken open with ax. (*Inspects the lock.*)

SCHOEN (*his hand on the door*): I suggest you prepare yourself.

ESCHERICH: If you'll be so kind as to open the door. . .

(SCHOEN *opens the door.*)

ESCHERICH (*drops his notebook and pencil, grasps at his hair*): Good God in Heaven. . . !

SCHOEN: I suggest you take a good look.

ESCHERICH: I can't!

SCHOEN (*looking scornfully at him*): Then may I ask why you came?

ESCHERICH: He c-c-cut his. . . throat with a ra-ra-razor. . .

SCHOEN: Are you finished?

ESCHERICH: What a terrible feeling that must be.

SCHOEN (*pulls the door shut, walks to the writing table*): Please sit down. Here's some paper and ink. Now write. . .

ESCHERICH (*who has sat down mechanically*): I can't write. . .

SCHOEN (*standing behind his chair*): Write! — Persecution mania. . .

ESCHERICH (*writing*): Per—sec—ution man—ni—a. . .

(*A bell rings in the hallway.*)

ACT THREE

A theater dressing room. The walls are red. A door upstage left. Upstage right, a Spanish screen. In the center is a long table, its end facing the audience. Dancing-costumes lie on it. Right and left of the table are armchairs. Downstage left, a small table with an armchair. Downstage right, a tall mirror; next to it a high-backed, very wide old-fashioned armchair. In front of the mirror, a pouf, make-up kits, etc., etc.

ALVA *is downstage left, filling two glasses with champagne and red wine.* LULU *is out of sight behind the Spanish screen.*

ALVA: All my years in the theatre and I've never seen so enthusiastic an audience.

LULU: Not too much red wine. — Will he see me today?

ALVA: My father?

LULU: Yes.

ALVA: I don't know if he's in the theatre.

LULU: Doesn't he care about seeing me?

ALVA: He hasn't much time.

LULU: His fiancee makes demands on him.

ALVA: He's speculating. He allows himself no rest. —

(DOCTOR SCHOEN *enters.*)

ALVA: Good God! We were just talking about you.

LULU: Is he here?

SCHOEN: Are you changing?

LULU (*looking over the Spanish screen; to* SCHOEN): You write in the papers I'm the most spirited dancer to set foot on the stage, that I'm a second Taglioni, and I don't know what, and yet not once have you found me gifted enough to come and convince yourself of the fact personally.

SCHOEN: I have so much writing to do. You see — I was correct. There was scarcely an empty seat. — You must learn to stay more downstage.

LULU: I must get used to the lights first.

ALVA: She stayed completely in character.

SCHOEN (*to* ALVA): You must learn to make more of your performers. You aren't yet in full command of the technique. (*To* LULU.) What do you play next?

LULU: A flower-girl...

SCHOEN (*to* ALVA): In tights?

ALVA: No. In an ankle-length dress.

SCHOEN: You'd have done better without the symbolism.

ALVA: I look at a dancer's feet.

SCHOEN: The important thing is what the audience looks

at. She's an apparition. She doesn't need your symbolic mummery. And thank God, too.

ALVA: It didn't seem to me the audience was bored.

SCHOEN: Of course not. But only because I've been working at her success in the papers for six months now.—Has the Prince been here?

ALVA: No one's been here.

SCHOEN: Who in his right mind lets a dancer come on for two whole acts in a raincoat!

ALVA: What Prince?

SCHOEN: Will I see you later?

ALVA: Are you alone?

SCHOEN: No, with friends.—At Peter's?

ALVA: At twelve?

SCHOEN: At twelve. (*He goes off.*)

LULU: I was beginning to doubt he'd ever come.

ALVA: Don't let his grumbling change your mind. Just save your energy for your final appearance.

(LULU *appears from behind the screen, dressed in a classical, ankle-length, sleeveless white dress with a red border, a multi-colored wreath on her head, and carrying a basket of flowers.*)

LULU: He didn't notice the clever use you made of your performers.

ALVA: A director doesn't put everything into the first act!

LULU (*the glass at her mouth*): You reveal me by degrees.

ALVA: Well, I suppose I knew you'd be good at costume changes.

LULU: If I'd sold flowers at the Café Alhambra like this, they'd have locked me up the first night.

ALVA: Why? You were just a child!

LULU: Do you remember the first time I entered your room?

ALVA (*nods*): You wore a dark blue dress with black velvet trim.

LULU: They had to hide me somewhere, but didn't know where.

ALVA: My mother had been sick in bed for two years. . .

LULU: You were playing theatre and asked me if I wanted to join in.

ALVA: That's right! We played theatre!

LULU: I can still see you moving the figures from one place to another.

ALVA: For a long time my most terrible memory was suddenly waking up and seeing the situation for what it was.

LULU: You turned very cold towards me then.

ALVA: My God — I saw in you something far superior to myself. I may have had a greater regard for you than for my own mother. Just imagine — when my mother died — I was only seventeen — I went straight to my father and demanded he marry you at once or we should have to fight a duel.

LULU: I know — he told me all about it.

ALVA: But now that I'm older, I can only pity him. He'll never understand me. He's drummed up some little plot in his head that has me opposing his marriage to the Countess.

LULU: Is she still as naïve as ever?

ALVA: She loves him. Or at least it looks that way to me. Her family's done everything to make her change her mind. I don't think there's any sacrifice too great for her where he's concerned.

LULU (*holds her glass out towards him*): May I have some more, please?

ALVA (*serving her*): You're drinking too much.

LULU: He must learn to believe in my success. He doesn't believe in any kind of art. All he believes in is newspapers.

ALVA: He doesn't believe in anything.

LULU: He brought me into the theatre so someone rich enough would come along and marry me.

ALVA: All right. But that's his problem, not ours.

LULU: I wouldn't mind dancing my way into a millionaire's heart.

ALVA: Heaven help us if anyone takes you away from us!

LULU: But you've already composed the music for it.

ALVA: You know I've always wanted to write a play for you.

LULU: But I'm not really meant for the stage.

ALVA: You were born a dancer.

LULU: You should write plays at least as interesting as life.

ALVA: No one would believe me.

LULU: I wonder what would have become of me if I hadn't understood more about acting than people on stage?

ALVA: I've packed your roles full of conceivable improbability.

LULU: That hocus-pocus doesn't hold water in real life.

ALVA: I'm satisfied just to see the public work itself into a frenzy.

LULU: I like seeing myself worked into a frenzy. (*She drinks.*)

ALVA: I'd say you're nearly there.

LULU: How can you doubt it, since my performance has a higher significance! There are people down there conferring very earnestly together.—I sense it, even though I can't see them.

ALVA: How do you sense it?

LULU: No one knows anything about anyone else. Everyone thinks himself the only unhappy victim.

ALVA: But how do you sense this?

LULU: You feel a cold shudder run down your spine.

ALVA: You're unbelievable. . .

(*An electric bell rings over the doorway.*)

LULU: My scarf. . . I'll remember to keep downstage.

ALVA (*placing a wide shawl around her shoulders*): Your scarf.

LULU: He won't have to worry about his shameless publicity again.

ALVA: Keep hold on yourself.

LULU: With God's help I'll dance the last spark of reason out of his head. (*She goes off.*)

ALVA (*alone*): A far more interesting play could certainly be written about her. (*He sits down, left, takes out a note-book and writes. Looking up.*) Act One: Doctor Goll. It's spoiled already. I could conjure up Doctor Goll from purgatory, or wherever he's expiating his orgies — but then I'd be held responsible for his sins. — (*Prolonged, loud, but muffled applause and cries of bravo are heard from outside.*) — It sounds like a menagerie at feeding time. — Act Two: Walter Schwarz. That's even more impossible. It's amazing how souls strip off the last veil in the blaze of such strokes of lightning! — Act Three? — How can it go on this way?! —

(*The dressing-room doors open from outside and* ESCERNY *enters. He acts as though at home, and without looking at* ALVA *takes a seat to the right of the mirror.*)

ALVA (*seated left, without looking at* ESCERNY): The third simply *can't* go on this way!

ESCERNY: It didn't seem to go as well today as usual — at least until the middle of the third act.

ALVA: I wasn't backstage.

ESCERNY: I had the pleasure of meeting her once at Doctor Schoen's.

ALVA: My father introduced her by means of some critiques in his paper.

ESCERNY (*bowing slightly*): I was conferring with Doctor Schoen about the publication of my explorations on Lake Tanganyika.

ALVA (*bowing slightly*): His remarks convince one of his lively interest in your work.

ESCERNY: It's refreshing how an audience doesn't exist for her.

ALVA: She learned the art of quick-change while still a child. But I was surprised to find her such an excellent dancer.

ESCERNY: When she dances her solo she becomes intoxicated with her own beauty — she seems mortally in love with it.

ALVA: Here she comes. (*He rises and opens the door.*)

(LULU *enters without her wreath and basket.*)

LULU (*to* ALVA): They're calling for you out there. I had three curtain-calls. (*To* ESCERNY.) Isn't Doctor Schoen in your box?

ESCERNY: Not in mine.

ALVA (*to* LULU): Didn't you see him?

LULU: He probably left.

ESCERNY: He's in the last box on the right.

LULU: He acts as though he's ashamed of me.

ALVA: That was the best seat he could get.

LULU (*to* ALVA): Be sure you ask him if he liked me better this time.

ALVA: I'll send him up.

ESCERNY: I saw him applaud.

LULU: Did you really?

ALVA: You'd better rest awhile. (*He goes off.*)

LULU: I'm afraid I have to change again.

ESCERNY: But your maid isn't here.

LULU: I do it faster myself. Where did you say Doctor Schoen was sitting?

ESCERNY: The last box on the right.

LULU: I still have five costume changes. Dancing-girl, ballerina, Queen of the Night, Ariel, and Lascaris. . . (*Slips behind the Spanish screen.*)

ESCERNY: Do you know that at our first meeting I expected to meet merely a young lady of the literary world? — (*Sits to the right of the center table, where he remains till the end of the scene.*) Am I wrong, or was I correct about the smile that thunderous applause brought to your lips? —— that you suffer from having to degrade your art in front of people of dubious interests? —— (*When* LULU *doesn't answer.*) That you would feel more at home in a villa richly furnished with every imaginable comfort — with unlimited means — so as to live completely as your own mistress?

(LULU *steps from behind the screen dressed in a*

short, bright pleated petticoat and white satin bodice, black shoes and stockings, and spurs on her heels. She is busy lacing her bodice.)

LULU: If I don't dance one evening I spend all night dreaming that I am, and the next morning I'm completely worn out. . .

ESCERNY: Imagine if instead of that rabble out there you had only *one* spectator, a *chosen* one.

LULU: It wouldn't make any difference. I never see anyone anyway.

ESCERNY: A lighted summer house — the plashing of waves from the lake below. . . On my exploration trips, you see, I'm forced to exercise a quite inhuman tyranny. . .

LULU (*in front of the mirror, putting on a pearl necklace*): That's a good school.

ESCERNY: And if I now want to deliver myself unconditionally into the power of a woman, then it's only the natural need for relaxation. . . What greater happiness for a woman than to have a man completely in her power?

LULU (*jingling her spurs*): Ah, yes!

ESCERNY (*confused*): There isn't an educated man alive who wouldn't go mad over you.

LULU: But who could live up to your wishes without deceiving you?

ESCERNY: A man would be ten times happier deceived by a girl like you than be loved honorably by anyone else.

LULU: You've never been loved honorably in your life. (*She turns her back to him and points at her bodice.*) Would you untie the knot for me? I tied it too tight. I'm always so excited when I dress.

ESCERNY (*after repeated attempts*): I'm sorry; I can't.

LULU: Leave it alone then. Maybe I can do it. (*She goes right.*)

ESCERNY: I confess a lack of deftness. Perhaps I didn't learn enough in my traffic with women.

LULU: I don't suppose you have much opportunity in Africa.

ESCERNY (*seriously*): I confess, my isolation in the world has embittered much of my life.

LULU: The knot's almost open. . .

ESCERNY: It's not your dancing that attracts me. It's the physical and spiritual refinement in your movements. Interested in art as I am, I couldn't be deceived in that. For ten evenings now I've studied your soul as expressed in your dancing. . . until today, when you came on stage as a flower-girl; then I knew I'd seen everything. You're very generous — unselfish. You can't bear to see others suffer. The embodiment of human happiness. You would make a man supremely happy as his wife. . . Your whole being is open-heartedness. — You would make a very poor actress. . .

(The electric bell rings over the door. — LULU has somewhat loosened the ties of her bodice, takes a deep breath, and jingles her spurs.)

LULU: I can breathe again. The curtain's going up. *(She takes a skirt-dance costume from the table — pleated light yellow silk, without a waist, high-necked, and with wide sleeves that reach to the knuckles — she throws it over her.)* I have to dance.

ESCERNY *(rises and kisses her hand)*: With your permission I'll stay here awhile longer.

LULU: Whatever you like.

ESCERNY: I need to be alone for awhile.

(LULU goes off.)

ESCERNY *(alone)*: What is nobility? — Eccentricity, like myself? — Or is it bodily and spiritual perfection, as in that girl? — *(Applause and shouts of bravo from outside become audible.)* The person who restores my faith in humanity will restore my life as well. — Shouldn't this woman's children have greater nobility of body and soul than the children of a woman who has as little vitality as I have shown until now? *(He sits downstage left; enthusiastically.)* Dance has ennobled her body. . .

(ALVA enters.)

ALVA: You never know when to expect an accident to ruin the whole performance! *(He throws himself into the armchair to the right of the mirror, so that the former position is exactly reversed. Their conversation is rather bored and apathetic.)*

ESCERNY: The public has never been so appreciative.

ALVA: She's finished the skirt-dance.

ESCERNY: I hear her coming...

ALVA: No, she's not.—She doesn't have time.—She changes costumes in the wings.

ESCERNY: Unless I'm mistaken, she has two ballerina costumes.

ALVA: I think the white one suits her better than the pink.

ESCERNY: Do you really?

ALVA: Don't you?

ESCERNY: I think the white tulle makes her look too bodiless.

ALVA: I think the pink tulle makes her look too animalistic.

ESCERNY: I don't think so.

ALVA: The white tulle brings out more the childlike quality of her nature.

ESCERNY: The rose tulle brings out more the womanly quality of her nature.

(The electric bell rings over the doorway.)

ALVA (*jumps up*): Good God, what's the matter!

ESCERNY (*rising simultaneously*): What is it?

(The electric bell rings through the end of the scene.)

ALVA: Something's happened...

ESCERNY: Why do you frighten so suddenly?

ALVA: Something terrible's gone wrong. (*He goes off.* ESCERNY *follows him.—The door remains open. The muffled strains of a waltz are heard.—Pause.*)

(LULU *enters in a long opera-cape, and pulls shut the door behind her. She wears a pink ballet costume with a garland of flowers, walks diagonally across the stage, and sits in the armchair beside the mirror.—Pause.*)

(ALVA *enters.*)

ALVA: Did you faint?

LULU: Please close the door.

ALVA: At least come down to the stage.

LULU: Did you see him?

ALVA: Did I see whom?

LULU: With his fiancee?

ALVA: With his. . . (*To* SCHOEN, *as he enters.*) You might have spared her that joke!

SCHOEN: What's the matter with her? (*To* LULU.) Won't you ever give up!

LULU: I feel as if I'd been whipped.

SCHOEN (*after locking the door*): You are going to dance—just as surely as I've taken responsibility for you!

LULU: In front of your fiancee?

SCHOEN: You have no right to question in front of whom! —You have a contract. You're being paid a salary. . .

LULU: That's none of your business!

SCHOEN: You will dance in front of anyone who buys a ticket. Your activities here have absolutely no connection with anyone who happens to be sitting in my box!

ALVA: Then I wish you'd *stayed* in your box! (*To* LULU.) Would you mind telling me what I'm to do!

(*A knock at the door from outside.*)

ALVA: That's the stage manager. (*Calls.*) Coming! Coming! Just a moment! (*To* LULU.) Are you forcing me to cancel the performance?

SCHOEN (*to* LULU): Get out on that stage!

LULU: Give me a moment! I can't right now. I feel deathly ill.

ALVA: Goddamn this whole business!

LULU: Start with the next number. No one will notice if I dance now or in five minutes. There's no strength in my feet.

ALVA: But you *will dance?*

LULU: As well as I can. . .

ALVA: As badly as you like. (*At the knocking heard again from outside.*) I'm coming! (Goes off.)

LULU: You're quite right putting me in my place. And what better way than making me dance in front of your fiancee . . . You do me a great service putting me in my place.

SCHOEN (*scornfully*): Considering your origins, you have extraordinary good fortune in being able to appear in front of respectable audiences!

LULU: Even when my shamelessness makes them not know where to look —

SCHOEN: That's ridiculous! — Shamelessness? — Don't make a necessity of virtue. — Every step of your shamelessness is paid its weight in gold. One shouts "Bravo!" and another "Shame!" — But to you they both mean the same thing. — What more brilliant a triumph could you hope for than when a perfectly respectable girl can scarcely be persuaded to stay in her box! What other aim have you in life! — As long as you have even a spark of self-respect you will never be a perfect dancer. The more you shock people, the higher your professional standing.

LULU: I couldn't begin to care what you think. Why should I want to be better than I am? I'm satisfied.

SCHOEN (*in moral indignation*): There's your true nature! Very honest of you, I must say. — Sheer corruption!

LULU: I never *knew* I had a spark of self-respect.

SCHOEN (*suddenly suspicious*): None of your tricks. . .

LULU: O God — I know very well what would have become of me if you hadn't saved me from it.

SCHOEN: Have you become anything else today?

LULU: No, thank God!

SCHOEN: Quite right.

LULU (*laughs*): And how insanely happy I am!

SCHOEN (*spits out*): Are you going to dance now?

LULU: *Any way* and in front of *any one!*

SCHOEN: Then get on stage!

LULU (*pleading like a child*): Just one more minute. Please. I can't quite stand yet. — They'll ring.

SCHOEN: So this is what you've come to, despite all I've sacrificed for your education and well being.

LULU (*ironically*): Could you have overrated your ennobling influence?

SCHOEN: You can spare me your witticisms!

LULU: The Prince was here.

SCHOEN: And?

LULU: He's taking me with him to Africa.

SCHOEN: Africa?!

LULU: Why not? Didn't you make a dancer of me so someone would come along and take me with him?

SCHOEN: But not to Africa!

LULU: Then why didn't you let me faint and silently thank heaven for it?

SCHOEN: Because, unfortunately, I had no reason to believe you really had fainted.

LULU (*contemptuously*): You couldn't bear it out there any longer. . . ?

SCHOEN: Because I had to convince you of who you are and to what you need not aspire!

LULU: Were you afraid my limbs might have been permanently damaged?

SCHOEN: I know too well how indestructible you are.

LULU: Oh, you know that, do you?

SCHOEN (*bursting out*): You needn't look at me with such impudence.

LULU: No one's keeping you.

SCHOEN: I'll leave when the bell rings.

LULU: What you mean is: as soon as you have the energy. — What's happened to your energy? — You've been engaged now for three years. Why don't you get married? — There's nothing holding you back. Why must you put the blame on me? — You demanded I marry Doctor Goll. I made Doctor Goll marry me. You demanded I marry the painter. I made the best of a bad bargain. — You create artists, you are the patron of princes. Why don't you get married?

SCHOEN (*raging*): I suppose you think *you're* standing in the way of it!

LULU (*exultantly from here to the end of the scene*): Oh, if you knew how happy your anger makes me! How proud I am that you humble me with every means at your disposal! You humiliate me as deeply as a man can humiliate a woman, because you think that then you can ignore me all the more easily. But you've suffered unspeakably for everything you've just said to me. I can see it in your face. Your self-control is almost at its end. Go on, get out! For the sake of your sweet, innocent fiancee, leave me alone! Another minute and your mood will change, and you'll bring on another scene that won't be as easy to justify!

SCHOEN: I'm not afraid of you anymore.

LULU: Me? — Be afraid of yourself! — I don't need you. — Will you please go? Don't hold me responsible. You know well enough I needn't faint to destroy your future. Your faith in my integrity knows no bounds! You don't believe I'm merely an enchanting creature; you also believe I'm one with a heart. I'm neither one nor the other. Your misfortune is that you think I am.

SCHOEN (*desperate*): Leave my thoughts alone. You already have two husbands underground. Take the Prince, dance him to destruction. I'm through with you. I know where the angel in you leaves off and the devil begins. If I accept the world as it is, then it's God who must answer for it, not I. Life is no amusement for me.

LULU: And yet you make greater demands upon life than anyone. Tell me, which of us asks more of life? You or I?

SCHOEN: Be quiet. I don't know how or what I think. When I listen to you I stop thinking altogether. I'll be married in eight days. I implore you — by the angel that is in you — not to cross my sight before then.

LULU: I'll lock my doors.

SCHOEN: Yes, go on, boast. — God as my witness, I have never in all my battle with life and the world cursed anyone as I have you.

LULU: That comes from my lowly origin.

SCHOEN: From your depravity!

Lulu: I accept the blame with infinite pleasure. How pure you must feel now. You must consider yourself a model of austerity, a paragon of unshakable principles — otherwise you could never marry that girl in her unfathomable innocence.

Schoen: Are you asking me to lay hands on you?

Lulu (*quickly*): Yes! Yes! What must I do to make you touch me! I wouldn't change places with that child now for a king's ransom! And yet the girl loves you as no woman has loved you yet!

Schoen: Be quiet! Monster! Quiet!

Lulu: Go on, marry her — and then in her childish misery she'll dance in front of *me* instead of me in front of *her!*

Schoen (*raises his fists*): God forgive me. . .

Lulu: Hit me. Where's your whip? Hit my legs!

Schoen (*hands at his temples*): I have to get out, get out. . . ! (*Rushes to the door, reflects, turns.*) Can I let the child see me this way? — I'll go home! — If only I could forget the world!

Lulu: Why not be a man? — Look yourself in the face for once. — There's not a trace of conscience in you. — There's no act despicable enough to frighten you. — You intend to make this girl who loves you miserable with all the coldbloodedness you have in you. — You conquer half the world. — You do whatever *you* like — and you know as well as I that. . .

Schoen (*completely exhausted, has collapsed in the armchair at left*): Stop!

Lulu: . . . that you are too weak — to tear yourself free of me. . .

Schoen (*groaning*): You're hurting me! You're hurting me!

Lulu: I can't tell you how happy I am at this moment!

Schoen: My age! My world!

Lulu: Crying like a child — that terrible and powerful man! — Go to your fiancee now and tell her what a splendid girl I am —and not one bit jealous!

Schoen (*sobbing*): That child! That innocent child!

Lulu: How can a devil incarnate suddenly become so weak? —— You will please go now. You mean nothing to me anymore.

SCHOEN: I can't go to her.

LULU: Get out of here! You can come back when you've recovered your strength.

SCHOEN: For God's sake, tell me what I'm to do!

(LULU *rises; her cape remains on the armchair. She pushes the costumes on the center table aside.*)

LULU: Here's some stationery...

SCHOEN: But I can't write...

LULU (*standing erect behind him, leaning on the back of his chair*): Write! — "My dear Miss. . ."

SCHOEN (*hesitantly*): I call her Adelaide...

LULU (*emphatically*): "My dear Miss..."

SCHOEN (*crying out*): — My death sentence!

LULU: "You must take back your promise. I cannot reconcile it" — (*as* SCHOEN *puts down the pen and looks at her*) — write it! — "*reconcile*" — "cannot reconcile it with my conscience to bind you to my unhappy lot. . ."

SCHOEN (*writing*): Yes. — Yes.

LULU: "I give you my word, that I am not worthy. . ." — (*as* SCHOEN *turns to her again*) — write it! —"not worthy" — "not worthy of your love. These words will prove it to you. For three years I have tried to tear myself loose; I haven't the strength. I write to you now by the side of the woman who masters me. — You must forget me. — Doctor Ludwig Schoen."

SCHOEN (*groaning aloud*): O God!

LULU (*half startled*): You needn't cry, "O God!" — (*With emphasis.*) "Doctor Ludwig Schoen." —"Postscript: You must make no attempt to rescue me."

SCHOEN (*collapses as he finishes writing*): Now — for — the — execution...

ACT FOUR

A magnificent hall decorated in German Renaissance style, with a heavy ceiling of carved oak. The lower half of the walls of dark carved wood; above them, on either side, are hung faded Gobelins. The upper rear of the room is cut off by a gallery hung with drapery; from it descends a monumental staircase which projects halfway downstage. In the center, beneath the gallery, is the entrance with its twisted columns and pediment. On the wall at right, a high and spacious French window leading onto a balcony; it is covered with heavy closed curtains. On the wall at the left, downstage of the staircase, a portiere of Genoese velvet.

A Chinese screen stands in front of the fireplace. LULU*'s picture as Pierrot, in an antiqued frame of gold, rests on a decorative easel situated in front of the outer bannister rail. Downstage left, a wide sofa; in front of it and to the right, an armchair. In the middle of the room stands a square table with a heavy covering. Around it are three highbacked upholstered chairs. A bouquet of white flowers is placed on the table.*

COUNTESS GESCHWITZ *is seated on the sofa; she is dressed in a fur-trimmed Hussar's jacket with a high stand-up collar, enormous cuff-links, and a veil over her face. Her hands are clasped convulsively in a muff.*

SCHOEN *stands downstage left.* LULU *is dressed in a large-flowered negligee. Her hair is in a simple knot, fastened by a gold clasp. She is seated in the armchair.*

GESCHWITZ (*to* LULU): I can't tell you how happy I am we'll see you at our ball for women artists.

SCHOEN: Is there no way for one of my sort to smuggle himself in?

GESCHWITZ: It were high treason to lend ourselves to such an intrigue.

SCHOEN (*walks behind the sofa to the center table*): What splendid flowers.

LULU: Countess Geschwitz brought them for me.

GESCHWITZ: Not at all, not at all.—You will, of course, come dressed as a man, won't you?

LULU: Do you think it suits me?

GESCHWITZ (*pointing at the portrait*): You're an absolute fairy tale in this.

LULU: My husband doesn't care for it.

GESCHWITZ: Is it by a local artist?

LULU: I don't think you'd have heard of him.

GESCHWITZ: Is he dead?

SCHOEN (*downstage right, with a deep voice*): He had all he could take.

LULU: You're not in a very good mood.

(SCHOEN *controls himself.*)

GESCHWITZ (*rising*): I'm afraid I must go, Madame. I mustn't stay any longer. We're having a life-class, and I still have so many preparations for the ball—(*Bowing.*) Doctor Schoen.

(LULU *leads her off through the center entrance.*)

SCHOEN (*alone, looking around*): And here we have the Augean stables. So this is the evening of my life. I dare anyone to show me a corner that's clean. There's the plague in this house. The poorest day-laborer has his tidy nest to come home to. Thirty years of work, and this is the family circle I have to show for it—the circle of those near and dear to me. . . (*He looks around.*) God knows who's eavesdropping on me now. (*He pulls a revolver from his breast pocket.*) No man can be certain of his own safety. (*The cocked revolver in his right hand, he walks over to the right and speaks into the drawn curtains.*) My family circle. That fellow still has some courage left.—

Wouldn't I be better off shooting myself in the head? — One can fight one's mortal enemies, but this. . . (*Draws the curtains aside; when he finds no one there*) . . . this filth — this filth. . . (*Shakes his head and walks left*) . . .either madness has taken possession of my sanity, or — exceptions prove the rule. (*Hearing* LULU, *he returns the revolver to his pocket.*)

LULU: Couldn't you be free this afternoon?

SCHOEN: What did the Countess want?

LULU: I don't know. She wants to paint me.

SCHOEN: Misfortune in human form comes to pay its respects.

LULU: Couldn't you try to be free? I'd like so much to take a ride with you through the grounds.

SCHOEN: You know I have to be at the Exchange. I'm never free today. Everything I own drifts on a sea of chance.

LULU: I'd rather be dead and buried than have my life so embittered by my property.

SCHOEN: Take life lightly and die easily.

LULU: Even as a child I had a terrible fear of death.

SCHOEN: Precisely why I married you.

LULU (*her arms around his neck*): You're in a terrible mood. You make so much trouble for yourself. I haven't seen anything of you for weeks and months.

SCHOEN (*stroking her hair*): Your lightness of heart must cheer my old age.

LULU: You didn't marry me.

SCHOEN: Whom did I marry then?

LULU: *I* married you.

SCHOEN: What difference does that make?

LULU: I'm afraid it makes a lot of difference.

SCHOEN: It's crushed a lot underfoot.

LULU: Except for one thing, thank God.

SCHOEN: And that is —?

LULU: Your love for me.

(SCHOEN *winces, signals her to walk ahead of him. Both go off downstage left.*)

(COUNTESS GESCHWITZ *cautiously opens the center door, ventures downstage and listens. She is startled when voices are heard in the gallery.*)

GESCHWITZ: O God, someone's there. . . (*She hides behind the screen in front of the fireplace.*)

SCHIGOLCH (*comes from behind the curtains onto the steps, turns back*): Did the boy leave his heart at the Night Light Cafe?!

RODRIGO (*between the curtains*): He's too young for the big world; he can't walk this far on foot yet. (*He disappears.*)

SCHIGOLCH (*comes down the steps*): Thank God we're finally home again. Some joker's waxed these steps. If I have to have any bones set in plaster again before I'm called home, she can prop me up between these palms and show me off to her relatives as the Venus de Medici. Shoals and pitfalls — shoals and pitfalls.

(RODRIGO *comes down the steps carrying* HUGENBERG *in his arms.*)

RODRIGO: This one here has a police chief for a father and no more guts than the raggediest beggar!

HUGENBERG: If it were a matter of life and death, you'd know what I'm made of soon enough.

RODRIGO: Our little brother here doesn't weigh more than sixty kilos, even with his lover's tears thrown in. I'll stake my life on that.

SCHIGOLCH: Throw him up to the ceiling and catch him by the feet. That'll start his blood going in the right direction.

HUGENBERG (*kicking his legs about*): Oh dear, oh dear, I'll be expelled from school.

RODRIGO (*setting him at the foot of the stairs*): You haven't been to a sensible school at all yet.

SCHIGOLCH: Many a man has won his spurs in this house. No need to be shy. First of all, I'll treat you to a drop of something that you can't buy for love or money. (*He opens a cabinet under the stairs.*)

HUGENBERG: Unless she dances in here in a split second I'm going to beat you silly.

RODRIGO (*has sat down to the right of the table*): Our little brother here's going to beat up the strongest man in the world. (*To* HUGENBERG.) Maybe him better go home first and let him mummy put him long pants on.

HUGENBERG (*sits down at left of the table*): I'd rather you loan me your moustache.

RODRIGO: You want her to throw you out of the house right away?

HUGENBERG: Damn, I wish I knew what to say to her!

RODRIGO: She knows that better than you.

SCHIGOLCH (*places two bottles and three glasses on the table*): I opened one of them yesterday. (*He fills the glasses.*)

RODRIGO (*guarding* HUGENBERG'*s glass*): Don't give him too much or we'll *both* be in for it.

SCHIGOLCH (*supporting himself with both hands on the top of the table*): Do you gentlemen smoke?

HUGENBERG (*opening his cigar-case*): Imported Havanas.

RODRIGO (*helping himself*): From your father the police chief?

SCHIGOLCH (*sitting down*): The house is well provisioned. You have only to ask.

HUGENBERG: I wrote her a poem yesterday.

RODRIGO: You wrote her *what?*

SCHIGOLCH: He wrote her *what?*

HUGENBERG: A poem.

RODRIGO (*to* SCHIGOLCH): A poem.

SCHIGOLCH: He's promised me a dollar if I find a place where they can meet alone.

HUGENBERG: Who lives here anyway?

RODRIGO: *We* live here!

SCHIGOLCH: Every Stock Exchange day we are at home here. — To your health!

(*They clink glasses.*)

HUGENBERG: Should I read it to you first?

SCHIGOLCH (*to* RODRIGO): What's he talking about?

RODRIGO: His poem. He'd like to try it on for size a little first.

SCHIGOLCH (*staring at* HUGENBERG): His eyes! His eyes!

RODRIGO: Yes, his eyes! They've robbed her of sleep for a whole week.

SCHIGOLCH (*to* RODRIGO): You might as well have yourself pickled.

RODRIGO: We *both* might as well have ourselves pickled. To your health, Old Father Death.

SCHIGOLCH (*touching glasses with him*): And to your health, old jack-in-the-box. If something better comes along later, I'll pull up stakes anytime, but. . . but. . .

(LULU *enters from the left dressed in an elegant Parisian ballgown with a deep décolleté, and with flowers at her breast and in her hair.*)

LULU: Oh, my dears, my dears, I'm expecting a visitor.

SCHIGOLCH: One thing I can say, they certainly know how to throw money around over there.

(HUGENBERG *has risen.*)

LULU (*sitting on the arm of his chair*): I must say, you've certainly got yourself in with a nice crowd. But, my dears, I'm expecting a visitor.

SCHIGOLCH: Well, I suppose I might as well put one on too. (*He looks among the flowers on the table.*)

LULU: Do I look nice?

SCHIGOLCH: What are those you're wearing in front?

LULU: Orchids. (*Leans her breasts towards* HUGENBERG.) Smell them.

RODRIGO: You must be expecting Prince Escerny.

LULU (*shakes her head*): God forbid!

RODRIGO: Another new one?!

LULU: The Prince is on a trip.

RODRIGO: To put his kingdom up for auction?

LULU: He's exploring a new tribe somewhere in Africa. (*She rises, rushes up the stairs and into the gallery.*)

RODRIGO (*to* SCHIGOLCH): — He once wanted to marry her.

SCHIGOLCH (*sticking a lily in his button-hole*): I also once wanted to marry her.

RODRIGO: You also once wanted to marry her?

SCHIGOLCH: Didn't *you* also once want to marry her?

RODRIGO: Of course I also once wanted to marry her.

SCHIGOLCH: Who *hasn't* also once wanted to marry her.

RODRIGO: I'd never have done better.

SCHIGOLCH: She's never let anyone regret not having married her.

RODRIGO: — Then she's not your daughter?

SCHIGOLCH: Never occurs to her.

HUGENBERG: Then what's her father's name?

SCHIGOLCH: She's bragged about me.

HUGENBERG: Then what's her father's name?

SCHIGOLCH: What did he say?

RODRIGO: What's her father's name?

SCHIGOLCH: She never had one.

(LULU *comes down out of the gallery and again sits on the arm of* HUGENBERG'S *chair.*)

LULU: What didn't I ever have?

ALL THREE: A father.

LULU: Of course. I'm a child prodigy. (*To* HUGENBERG.) How satisfied are you with *your* father?

RODRIGO: At least the police chief smokes a respectable cigar.

SCHIGOLCH: Have you locked the upstairs door?

LULU: Here's the key.

SCHIGOLCH: You should have left it in the lock.

LULU: Why?

SCHIGOLCH: So it can't be unlocked from outside.

RODRIGO: Isn't he at the Exchange?

LULU: Yes, of course, but he suffers from a persecution mania.

RODRIGO: I'll take him by the feet, and pow! He'll be sticking to the ceiling.

LULU: He could chase you into a mousehole with a quarter of a side glance.

RODRIGO: Chase *what?* Who's he going to chase? (*He bares his arm.*) Take a look at those biceps.

LULU: Let's see. (*Goes to the right.*)

RODRIGO (*striking himself on the arms*): Solid granite! — Cast iron!

LULU (*feels* RODRIGO'S *arm, and then her own*): If only you didn't have such long ears. . .

FERDINAND (*enters through the center door*): Doctor Schoen.

RODRIGO (*jumping up*): The bastard! (*Starts to hide behind the screen in front of the fireplace; recoils.*) God preserve us! (*Hides downstage left behind the curtains.*)

SCHIGOLCH: Give me the key! (*Takes the key from* LULU *and drags himself up the stairs to the gallery.*)

(HUGENBERG *has slid from the chair under the table.*)

LULU: You may show him in.

(FERDINAND *goes out.*)

HUGENBERG (*looking out and listening from under the table; to himself*): I hope he doesn't stay — then we'll be alone. . .

(LULU *touches him with the tip of her shoe.* HUGENBERG *disappears.*)
(FERDINAND *shows in* ALVA, *then goes off.*)

ALVA (*in evening dress*): I suspect the matinee will play by artificial light. I have. . . (*Noting* SCHIGOLCH *laboriously dragging himself up the stairs.*) What's that?

LULU: An old friend of your father's.

ALVA: Never met him in my life.

LULU: They served together in the war. He's having a terrible time of it...

ALVA: Is my father here?

LULU: He had a drink with him. He had to go to the Exchange. — We're going to have lunch first, aren't we?

ALVA: When does it start?

LULU: After two. (*As* ALVA *follows* SCHIGOLCH *with his eyes.*) What do you think of me?

(SCHIGOLCH *goes off through the gallery.*)

ALVA: Hadn't I best keep quiet on that subject?

LULU: I mean, how do I look?

ALVA: Your dressmaker obviously knows you better than I... should ever allow myself to.

LULU: Looking at myself in the mirror I wished I were a man... my own husband. —

ALVA: You envy your husband the happiness you offer him.

(LULU *is at left,* ALVA *at the right of the center table. He looks at her with shy satisfaction.*)

(FERDINAND *enters through the middle door with two place settings, which he arranges on the table along with a bottle of Pommery and hors d'oeuvres.*)

ALVA (*to* FERDINAND): Do you have a toothache?

LULU (*across to* ALVA): Don't.

FERDINAND: Doctor...?

ALVA: He seems so weepy today.

FERDINAND (*through his teeth*): I'm only human.—— (*Goes off.*)

(*They both sit at the table.*)

LULU: — What I've always admired most about you is your firmness of character. You're so sure of yourself. Even when you must have been afraid of arguing with your father, you always stood up for me like a little brother.

ALVA: Let's drop the subject. — It's been my fate. . . (*He is about to lift the front of the tablecloth.*)

LULU (*quickly*): That was me.

ALVA: Impossible. — It's been my fate to always achieve the very best while harboring the most frivolous ideas.

LULU: Thinking yourself evil does you an injustice.

ALVA: Why do you flatter me like this? — There's no more wicked man alive, who — who has brought so much good into the world.

LULU: You're the only man in the world who's ever protected me without debasing me in my own eyes.

ALVA: You think that's been easy. . .?

(SCHOEN *appears in the gallery between the two middle columns while cautiously parting the curtains.*)

SCHOEN (*in a stage whisper*): My own son!

ALVA: . . .With such God-given gifts as yours one makes criminals of those around him without realizing it. — I'm only flesh and blood, too, and if we hadn't been raised as brother and sister. . .

LULU: That's why you're the only one I can be at ease with. I have no reason to be afraid of you.

ALVA: There are moments when one expects to see his whole inner being collapse. — The more self-constraint a man assumes, the more easily he goes to pieces. There's no way out of it except. . . (*He acts as if about to look under the table.*)

LULU (*quietly*): What are you looking for?

ALVA: Please, let me keep my confessions to myself. You were more to me as an inviolable sanctuary than with all your gifts you could ever be to anyone else!

LULU: You do look at it differently than your father.

(FERDINAND *enters through the middle door, changes the plates, and serves roast chicken and salad.*)

ALVA (*to* FERDINAND): Are you ill?

LULU (*to* ALVA): Will you leave him alone.

ALVA: He's trembling as though he had a fever.

FERDINAND: I'm not accustomed to serving at table.

ALVA: You ought to have a doctor prescribe something.

FERDINAND (*through his teeth*): I'm generally the coachman. —— (*He goes off.*)

SCHOEN (*speaks in a stage whisper from the gallery*): So he's another one. (*He stands behind the balustrade, hiding behind the curtain when necessary.*)

LULU: You said there were moments when one expects to see his whole inner being collapse — what are they like?

ALVA: I really didn't want to talk about them. — I'd rather not jest over a glass of champagne about my life's greatest happiness these last ten years.

LULU: I've hurt you. I won't bring it up again.

ALVA: Is that a life-long promise?

LULU: My hand on it. (*She extends her hand to him across the table.*)

(ALVA *takes hold of it hesitantly, presses it in his own, and then presses it long and ardently to his lips.*)

LULU: What are you doing. . .

(RODRIGO *sticks his head through the curtain at right.* LULU *throws him an angry look across* ALVA. RODRIGO *withdraws.*)

SCHOEN (*speaks in a stage whisper from the gallery*): And there's another!

ALVA (*holding her hand*): A soul — rubbing the sleep from his eyes in the next world. . . O this hand. . .

LULU (*innocently*): What do you see in it. . .

ALVA: An arm. . .

LULU: What do you see in it. . .

ALVA: A body. . .

LULU (*guilelessly*): What do you see in it. . .

ALVA (*aroused*): Mignon!

LULU (*quite uncomprehendingly*): What do you see in it. . .

ALVA (*passionately*): Mignon! Mignon!

LULU (*throws herself onto the ottoman*): Don't look at me like that — for God's sake! Why don't we leave before it's too late. You're a terrible person!

ALVA: I told you I was the basest of scoundrels. . .

LULU: Yes, I can see.

ALVA: I have no sense of honor — no pride. . .

LULU: And you take me for one of your kind?

ALVA: You? — You are as high above me as — as the sun towering over an abyss. . . (*Kneeling.*) Destroy me! — I beg of you, put an end to me! — Put an end to me!

LULU: Do you love me?

ALVA: I'll pay for you with everything that was mine!

LULU: Do you love me?

ALVA: Do you love me — Mignon. . .?

LULU: I? — I love no one.

ALVA: I love you. (*Nestles his head in her lap.*)

LULU (*her hand in his hair*): — I poisoned your mother.

(RODRIGO *sticks his head through the curtains at right, sees* SCHOEN *sitting in the gallery and motions to draw his attention to* LULU *and* ALVA. SCHOEN *points his revolver at* RODRIGO. RODRIGO *signals him to point it at* ALVA. SCHOEN *cocks the weapon and aims it at* RODRIGO. RODRIGO *withdraws behind the curtains.* LULU *sees* RODRIGO *withdraw, sees* SCHOEN *sitting in the gallery, and rises.*)

LULU: His father!

(SCHOEN *rises, lets the curtain fall in front of him.* ALVA *remains motionless on his knees. — Pause. —* SCHOEN, *a newspaper in hand, takes* ALVA *by the shoulder.*)

SCHOEN: Alva!

(ALVA *rises as though drunk with sleep.*)

SCHOEN: A revolution has broken out in Paris.

ALVA: To Paris. . . let me go to Paris. . .

SCHOEN: They're beating their heads against the wall at the newspaper office. No one knows what to write. . . (*He unfolds the newspaper, leads* ALVA *off through the middle door.* — RODRIGO *bursts from behind the curtain at right and runs for the stairs.* LULU *bars his way.*)

LULU: You can't get out this way.

RODRIGO: Let me through!

LULU: You'll run right into his arms.

RODRIGO: He'll put a bullet through my head!

LULU: He's coming.

RODRIGO (*running back*): O hell o hell o hell! (*Lifts the tablecloth.*)

HUGENBERG: All filled up.

RODRIGO: My God, I'm washed up! (*Looks around, hides at left behind the portiere.*)

(SCHOEN *enters through the middle door, locks it, and, with the revolver in his hand, goes to the window downstage right. He raises the curtains.*)

SCHOEN: — Where did he go?

LULU (*on the bottom step*): Out.

SCHOEN: Over the balcony?

LULU: He's an acrobat.

SCHOEN: No way of foreseeing that, I suppose. — (*Turning towards* LULU.) You — drag me through the gutter to a martyr's death!

LULU: Why didn't you bring me up better?

SCHOEN: You are a destroying angel. You are inexorable fate. — Become a murderer or drown in filth; run off to sea like a criminal set free or hang myself over the morass. Joy of my old age. My hangman's noose.

LULU (*coldbloodedly*): Shut up and kill me.

SCHOEN: I've signed over everything to you and asked nothing in return but the respect which a mere servant ought to show for my house. Your credit has been exhausted.

LULU: I can give security for my account for years to come. (*Coming downstage from the stairs.*) How do you like my new dress?

SCHOEN: Get out of here. Or by tomorrow I may go mad and find my son swimming in his own blood. You've laid hold of me like some incurable plague that I must endure till the day I die. I want to cure myself. Do you understand? (*Forcing the revolver on her.*) This is the medicine. — Don't go weak at the knees. — You're to apply it to yourself. You or I — which of us is stronger?

(LULU *has sat down on the divan as her strength threatened to leave her. She turns the revolver from side to side.*)

LULU: This won't go off.

SCHOEN: Do you remember how I tore you from the clutches of the police?

LULU: You're very trusting. . .

SCHOEN: Because I'm not afraid of a whore? Shall I guide your hand for you? Have you no pity for yourself? (*As* LULU *points the revolver at him.*) No false alarms.

(LULU *fires a shot at the ceiling.* RODRIGO *jumps from behind the portiere and runs up the stairs and across the gallery.*)

SCHOEN: What was that?

LULU (*innocently*): Nothing.

SCHOEN (*lifting the portieres*): Who flew out of here?

LULU: It's your persecution mania.

SCHOEN: Do you have any more men hidden here? (*Tearing the revolver from her.*) Are there any more men visiting you? (*Going towards the right.*) I'd like to entertain your men. (*Throws open the curtains, tosses aside the fire-screen, grasps* GESCHWITZ *by the collar and drags her downstage.*) Did you come down through the chimney?

GESCHWITZ (*to* LULU, *in mortal fear*): Save me!

SCHOEN (*shaking her*): Or are you an acrobat, too?

GESCHWITZ (*whimpering*): You're hurting me.

SCHOEN (*shaking her*): You really must stay for dinner. (*Drags her left, pushes her into the neighboring room, and locks the door after her.*) We don't need publicity. (*Sits beside* LULU, *forces the revolver on her.*) There's still enough in it for you. — Look at me! I can't let my own coachman decorate my forehead for me in my own house. Look at me! I pay my coachman. Look at me! Am I doing my coachman a favor when I can't bear the disgusting stench of the stables?

LULU: Order the carriage. Please. We're going to the opera.

SCHOEN: We're going to the devil! Now I'm the coachman. (*He aims the revolver in her hand away from himself and at* LULU'*s breast.*) Do you really believe anyone would allow himself to be mistreated as you've mistreated me, and then weigh the disgrace of going to prison against the public service of ridding the world of a creature like you? (*He holds her down by the arm.*) Let's put an end to it. It will be the happiest recollection of my life. Fire!

LULU: — You can get a divorce.

SCHOEN (*rising*): That's all there is. So that tomorrow my successor can find his pastime where I have shuddered from chasm to chasm with suicide at my back and you in front of me. How can you dare to say such a thing. Am I to see that part of my life which I made yours thrown to wild beasts? Can you see your bed with the sacrificial victim on it? The boy is homesick for you. — Did you get a divorce? You've trampled him underfoot, beat out his brains, and caught his blood in gold pieces. Me get a divorce! Is divorce possible when two people have grown so together that half of him is cut off in the division? (*Reaching for the revolver.*) Give it to me.

LULU: Have mercy on me!

SCHOEN: I want to spare you the trouble.

LULU (*breaks from him, holding the revolver down; in a determined, self-confident tone*): — If men have killed themselves for me, that can't lower my value. — You know as well why you made me your wife as I knew why I took you for a husband. — You betrayed your best friends with me, and you couldn't very well continue betraying yourself with me. — If you've brought me the evening of your life as an offering, then remember I gave you my youth for it. You knew ten times better than I which is of greater value. I have never in my life wanted to appear other than what people have thought me; and no one has ever in my life thought me to be other than what I am. — You're trying to force me to put a bullet through my heart. — I may not be sixteen anymore, but I'm still too young to put a bullet through my heart.

SCHOEN (*closing in on her*): Down, murderess! Down! On your knees — murderess! (*He forces her to the steps. Raising his head.*) Down — and don't dare stand up again!

(LULU *has sunk to her knees.*)

SCHOEN: Murderess — pray God to give you strength. Beg Heaven to give you strength for it!

HUGENBERG (*jumping up from beneath the table and pushing the chair aside*): Help!

(SCHOEN *turns towards* HUGENBERG, *turning his back on* LULU. LULU *fires five shots at* SCHOEN, *and continues pulling the trigger.*)

SCHOEN (*falling forward is caught by* HUGENBERG, *who lowers him into the chair*): And — there — is — one — more. . .

LULU (*rushing to* SCHOEN): Merciful Heaven. . .

SCHOEN: Out of my sight! ——— Alva!

LULU (*on her knees*): The only man I ever loved!

SCHOEN: Whore! Murderess! — Alva! Alva! — Water!

LULU: Water — he's thirsty. (*She fills a glass with champagne and puts it to* SCHOEN'S *lips.*)

ALVA (*entering through the gallery and coming down the stairs*): Father! For God's sake! Father!

LULU: I shot him.

HUGENBERG: She's innocent!

SCHOEN (*to* ALVA): She's yours. I've failed.

ALVA (*tries to lift him*): You've got to get to bed. Come.

SCHOEN: Don't grab me like that. — I'm drying up. . .

(LULU *comes with the champagne glass.*)

SCHOEN (*to* LULU): You haven't changed. (*After having drunk; to* ALVA.) Don't let her escape. — You're the next one. . .

ALVA (*to* HUGENBERG): Take hold of him. (*Indicating towards the left.*) The bedroom.

(*They both raise* SCHOEN *up and lead him toward the right, glass in hand.*)

SCHOEN (*groaning*): O God, o God, o God. . .

(ALVA *finds the door locked, turns the key and opens it.* COUNTESS GESCHWITZ *comes out.*)

SCHOEN (*pulls himself up stiffly at sight of her*): The Devil — (*Falls backward onto the carpet.*)

LULU (*throws herself down beside him, takes his head on her lap, kisses him*): It's all over. (*She straightens up, about to go towards the steps.*)

ALVA: Stay here! —

GESCHWITZ (*to* LULU): I thought it was you.

LULU (*throwing herself down in front of* ALVA): You can't turn me over to the law. It's my head they'll cut off. I shot him because he'd have shot me. I never loved anyone in the world but him. Ask anything of me you like, Alva. Don't let me fall into the hands of the law. It would be such a pity. I'm still so young. I'll be faithful to you all my life. I'll belong to no one but you. Look at me, Alva. — Alva, look at me! Look at me!

(*Knocking is heard from outside.*)

ALVA: The police. (*Goes to open the door for them.*)

HUGENBERG: I'll be expelled from school!

PANDORA'S BOX

A Tragedy in Three Acts

CAST OF CHARACTERS

LULU
ALVA SCHOEN, a writer
RODRIGO QUAST, an acrobat
SCHIGOLCH
ALFRED HUGENBERG, inmate of a reformatory
COUNTESS GESCHWITZ
MARQUIS CASTI-PIANI
PUNTSCHU, a banker
HEILMANN, a journalist
MAGELONE
KADIDJA DI SANTA CROCE, her daughter
BIANETTA GAZIL
LUDMILLA STEINHERZ
BOB, a groom
A POLICE INSPECTOR
MR. HUNIDEI
KUNGU POTI, Crown Prince of Uahubee
DOCTOR HILTI, a university lecturer
JACK

PLACE:

The first act takes place in Germany, the second in Paris, and the third in London.

ACT ONE

A magnificent hall decorated in German Renaissance style, with a heavy ceiling of carved oak. The lower half of the walls are of dark carved wood; above them on either side are hung faded Gobelins. The upper rear of the room is cut off by a gallery hung with draperies; from it descends a monumental staircase, left, which projects halfway downstage. In the center, beneath the gallery, is the entrance with its twisted columns and pediment. On the wall at the right, a high and spacious fireplace. Farther downstage is a French window leading onto a balcony; it is covered with heavy closed curtains. On the wall at the left, downstage of the staircase, a portiere. Situated near the front of the staircase stands an empty decorative easel. Downstage left is a wide sofa, and in the center of the room a square table with three highback upholstered chairs around it. Downstage left is a small serving-table; beside it, a reclining-chair. The room is dimly lighted by a heavily shaded oil-lamp on a center table. ALVA SCHOEN *paces back and forth in front of the entrance.* RODRIGO, *dressed as a servant, sits on the sofa.* COUNTESS GESCHWITZ, *in a black, close-fitting dress, sits in the reclining-chair at right, deep in cushions and with a rug over her knees. A coffee-machine and a cup of black coffee are on the table beside her. — Left and right are from the audience's point of view.*

RODRIGO: You'd think he was a symphony conductor, the way he keeps people waiting.

GESCHWITZ: Will you please not talk.

RODRIGO: How's a person with a head full of ideas supposed

to keep his trap shut? — I don't understand how she could have been bettered by it.

GESCHWITZ: She's more magnificent to look at than I have ever known her.

RODRIGO: God help me from founding my happiness on *your* sense of beauty. If the sickness had the same effect on her as on you, I'm washed up. You came out of the isolation ward looking like a fat lady at the circus who's been on a hunger strike. It's all you can do to blow your nose. You need a quarter of an hour to sort out your fingers and it takes a great deal of care for you not to break off the tips.

GESCHWITZ: What sends us to our graves, gives her renewed strength and vitality.

RODRIGO: That's all very well, but I don't think I'll be going with her this evening.

GESCHWITZ: You're letting your fiancee travel alone?

RODRIGO: The old man will be with her to defend her if necessary. My going along would only look suspicious. Besides, I have to wait here for my costumes to be finished. — I'll get across the border soon enough. In the meantime let's hope she puts on a little flesh. Then there'll be the wedding, provided, of course, I can present her to a respectable audience. I like women to be practical; whatever theories they devise for themselves means nothing to me. Do you agree, Doctor Schoen?

ALVA: I didn't hear you.

RODRIGO: I'd never have got mixed up in this plot if she hadn't made advances to me before going to jail. I hope she doesn't start doing too much the minute she's out of the country. I'd like to take her to London for six months and let her eat plum cakes. Sea air swells a person up. And in London you don't feel the hand of fate at your throat every time you take a drink of beer.

ALVA: I've wondered for a week now whether one sent up to jail can still play the leading role in a modern drama.

GESCHWITZ: I wish to Heaven he'd come.

RODRIGO: I still have to redeem my props from the pawn shop; six hundred kilos of the best iron. It costs me three times more to ship them than my own ticket — which means the whole deal isn't worth a hill of beans. When I lugged them into the pawn shop, sweating like a dog, they asked me if they were genuine. — I should have had my costumes made abroad. In Paris they know right off what a man's best points are and lay them bare without shame. You don't learn that by sitting back with your legs crossed; you learn it by studying with men of classical education. They're as scared of bare skin in this country as they are abroad of bombs. Two years ago I was fined fifty Marks at the Alhambra Theatre because you could see the few hairs on my chest — really not enough to make a respectable toothbrush. The Ministry of Culture was afraid it would cause school girls to lose interest in knitting stockings. Since then I've had myself shaved once a month.

ALVA: If I didn't need all my intellectual energy now for my play, *The Ruler of the World*, I'd like to test that problem for its drawing power. The trouble with literature today is we're too literary. The only problems we know are those that arise among writers and scholars. Our interests are limited by our immediate professional interests. To return to great and powerful art we must concern ourselves with people who have never in their lives read a book, whose simple animal instincts determine everything they do. In my play, *Earth Spirit*, I did my best to live up to these principles. The female lead in that play has spent the past year behind iron bars. And so, for some incomprehensible reason, the play was produced only by an enlightened literary society. While my father was still alive my plays were welcome all over Germany. But it seems times have changed.

RODRIGO: I had a pair of tights made of the most delicate shade of bluish-green. If they don't cause a sensation abroad I'll settle down to selling mousetraps. The trunks are so tiny I wouldn't dare sit down on the edge of a table. The only bad thing is this paunch of mine. I thank my active participation in this conspiracy for that. Lying in the hospital for three months, in perfect health, would have made the most broken-down tramp look like a hog. Since I've been out all I've eaten is Karlsbad pills. I have an orchestra rehearsing in my guts day and night. By the time I cross the border I'll be so flushed out I won't even be able to lift a cork.

GESCHWITZ: It was cheering yesterday to see those hospital attendants keep out of her way. The garden was as quiet as a grave. The convalescents didn't dare venture out into the most magnificent noonday sun. At the rear by the isolation ward *she* appeared beneath the mulberry trees and swayed to and fro on the gravel. The door-keeper recognized me, and the intern who met me in the corridor jumped as if he'd been shot. The sisters stole through the enormous rooms or hugged the walls. When I returned, I saw no one in the garden or at the gate. There couldn't have been a better time, if only we'd had those blasted passports. And now *this* creature says he's not going along!

RODRIGO: I understand those poor hospital boys all right. The one has a sore foot, the other a swollen cheek; then suddenly a death-insurance agent pops up in front of them. When I spread the news of Sister Theophila's death, you should have seen the ward we called the Hall of Knights, — it was also the place I conducted my investigations from. You couldn't keep those bastards in bed. They climbed up the barred windows carrying their pains by the hundredweight. I never heard such swearing in all my life.

ALVA: You will allow me, Countess, to return to my former proposition. Despite the fact she shot my father in this room, I see both the murder and her punishment as nothing but a horrible misfortune. And I don't believe that if my father had lived he would have withdrawn his support of her entirely. Your plan to free her seems a bit doubtful: though I shouldn't want to discourage you. Your self-sacrifice, your industry, your super-human scorn of death are a great inspiration to me. I don't think any man has ever risked so much for a woman, not to mention for a friend. I have no idea how wealthy you are, Countess Geschwitz, but the expense of this plan must certainly have exhausted your fortune. I can offer you a loan of, say, twenty thousand Marks. I should have no trouble raising that in cash.

GESCHWITZ: Oh, how we rejoiced when Sister Theophila was finally dead! From that day on we had no supervision whatever. We changed beds whenever we wanted. I did her hair like mine and copied every inflection of her voice. When the professor came he addressed her as "my dear Countess," and to me he said, "It's better here than in prison!" — Since the sister was suddenly absent, we looked at each other in suspense; we had both been sick for five days; and now was the deciding moment. The next morning the intern came. — "How is Sister Theophila?" — "Dead." — We communicated behind his back, and when he had gone we fell into each other's arms and cried: "Thank God! Thank God!" — Oh, and the trouble I had keeping my darling from showing how well she already was! — "You have nine years of jail ahead of you!" I cried at her from morning till night. — Now they probably won't let her stay in the isolation ward more than three more days.

RODRIGO: I lay in the hospital for three whole months just getting the lay of the place — after laboriously gathering together the qualities necessary to make so prolonged a stay possible. I now serve here as your valet, Doctor Schoen, to see no strange servants come into your house. When has a bridegroom done more for his bride? And my fortune has been exhausted.

ALVA: If you succeed in making a respectable artist of her you'll have put the world in your debt. The temperament and beauty of her inner-self can make the most blasé audience hold its breath. And then, of course, she'll be protected from actually becoming a criminal again by simulating passion on stage.

RODRIGO: I'll teach her how not to play pranks!

GESCHWITZ: Here he comes.

(Footsteps are heard in the gallery; then the curtains part and SCHIGOLCH *enters in a long black frock coat, and holding a white umbrella in his right hand. Throughout the play his speech is interrupted by frequent yawning.)*

SCHIGOLCH: Damned darkness! — Outside the sun burns your eyes out.

GESCHWITZ *(wearily unwrapping herself from the rug)*: I'm coming!

RODRIGO: Her ladyship hasn't seen a ray of light for three days. We might as well live in a snuff-box.

SCHIGOLCH: Since nine this morning I've made the rounds of all the rag-pickers. I've sent three new trunks stuffed with old pants to Buenos Aires via Bremerhaven by express. My legs dangle from my body like the clappers of a bell. But it's all going to be different from now on.

RODRIGO: Where are you getting off tomorrow morning?

SCHIGOLCH: In any case let's hope I won't be living at government expense again.

RODRIGO: I can recommend an excellent hotel. I lived there once with a lady lion tamer. The people were born in Berlin.

GESCHWITZ *(sitting up in her chair)*: Will you please help me!

RODRIGO *(hurries over and supports her)*: And you'll be safer there from the police than on a mile high tightrope.

GESCHWITZ: He intends you two to leave together this afternoon.

SCHIGOLCH: He's probably still suffering from frostbite.

RODRIGO: Do you expect me to make my debut in bathrobe and slippers?

SCHIGOLCH: Hm. — Sister Theophila wouldn't have gone to Heaven quite so promptly if she hadn't taken such a loving interest in our patient.

RODRIGO: There'll have to be changes if anyone's to live through a honeymoon with *her*. But it can't harm her any if she airs herself out a bit.

ALVA (*holds a briefcase while talking to* GESCHWITZ, *who stands at the center table, supporting herself by the arm of a chair*): There are ten thousand Marks in this briefcase.

GESCHWITZ: Thank you, no.

ALVA: I beg you, take them.

GESCHWITZ (*to* SCHIGOLCH): Will you please hurry!

SCHIGOLCH: Patience, Countess, patience. Hospital Street is only a stone's throw away. — I'll be back with her in five minutes.

ALVA: You're bringing her here?

SCHIGOLCH: I'm bringing her here. — Or do you fear for your health?

ALVA: You can see perfectly well that I'm afraid of nothing.

RODRIGO: According to the latest news releases, Doctor Schoen is on his way to Constantinople to have his *Earth Spirit* played for the Sultan by concubines and eunuchs.

ALVA (*opening the center door under the gallery*): This way is quicker.

(SCHIGOLCH *and* COUNTESS GESCHWITZ *leave the room.* ALVA *locks the door behind them.*)

RODRIGO: You wanted to give that crazy female money.

ALVA: That's none of your business.

RODRIGO: I'm paid like a lamp-cleaner, despite the fact I had to demoralize all the sisters in the hospital. Not to mention the interns, and professors, and. . .

ALVA: Are you trying to tell me you influenced the professors too?

RODRIGO: The money they cost me could have made me President of the United States.

ALVA: Countess Geschwitz reimbursed you for every penny you spent. And unless I'm mistaken, you're getting a salary from her of five hundred Marks a month. At times I don't quite believe in your love for our little murderess. When I offered the Countess my assistance, just now, it wasn't to arouse your insatiable lust for money. My admiration for you in this regard is far from what I feel for the Countess. Besides, I have no idea what claims you think you have on me. Your presence at my father's murder is no reason for any relationship between us. But I know one thing: if Countess Geschwitz and her heroic plan hadn't come your way, you'd be lying in the gutter without a penny to your name.

RODRIGO: And do you know what would have happened to you if you hadn't sold that miserable little paper of your father's for two million? — You'd have gotten mixed up with the most emaciated ballet dancer imaginable; you'd be a stable boy with the Humplemeier Circus. What work do you do? — You've written a horror play with my fiancee's calves as the two leading characters and that no theatre will produce. You crazy fool! You miserable worm! Two years ago I was balancing two saddled cavalry horses on my chest. How I'll get on with this paunch remains to be seen. Imagine the impression of German artistry those foreign women will get when they see beads of sweat oozing from my tights with every pound I lift. I'll pollute the whole auditorium with my stink.

ALVA: You're a weakling.

RODRIGO: I wish to hell you were right. Or were you trying to insult me? — If so, I'll give you a kick that'll send your tongue across the carpet.

ALVA: Try it.

(Footsteps and voices are heard from off.)

ALVA: Who's that. . .?

RODRIGO: You can thank God there's no audience here.

ALVA: Who can it be?

RODRIGO: My fiancee. We haven't seen each other for a whole year.

ALVA: How could they be back so soon? — Who can have come? — I'm not expecting anyone.

RODRIGO: Damnation, will you open the door or not!

ALVA: Hide!

RODRIGO: I'll stand behind the portieres. It's also been a year since *I* stood behind *them*. (RODRIGO *disappears behind the portieres downstage left.*)

(ALVA *opens the door, and* ALFRED HUGENBERG, *hat in hand, enters.*)

ALVA: Whom have I the. . . You? — Aren't you. . . ?

HUGENBERG: Alfred Hugenberg.

ALVA: What is it you want?

HUGENBERG: I've just arrived from Muensterberg. I escaped this morning.

ALVA: I have eye trouble. I'm supposed to keep the blinds drawn.

HUGENBERG: I need your help. You won't refuse me. I've devised a plan. — Can anyone hear us?

ALVA: What are you talking about? — What kind of a plan?

HUGENBERG: Are you here alone?

ALVA: Yes. — What are you trying to tell me?

HUGENBERG: I've already scrapped two of the plans. What I'm about to tell you has been worked out to the minutest degree. If I had money I wouldn't be drawing you into my confidence. I thought about it for a long time at first. . . — May I explain my plan to you?

ALVA: Would you mind telling me first what you're talking about?

HUGENBERG: Do you care so little about her that I have to explain it? The evidence you gave the examining magistrate helped her more than everything the defense counsel said.

ALVA: I beg to decline any such insinuation.

HUGENBERG: You'd say that in any case; I understand. And yet you were the best witness for the defense.

ALVA: No, *you* were! You said my father was trying to force her to shoot herself.

HUGENBERG: He was, too. But no one believed me. I wasn't sworn in.

ALVA: Where have you just come from?

HUGENBERG: From a reformatory. I broke out this morning.

ALVA: What do you intend to do?

HUGENBERG: Gain the confidence of a turnkey.

ALVA: What will you live off of?

HUGENBERG: I'm living with a girl who has a child by my father.

ALVA: Who is your father?

HUGENBERG: Police chief. I know the prison without having been inside; no one will recognize me the way I look now. But I'm not counting on that. I know of an iron ladder that leads from the first court-yard onto the roof and through a skylight into the attic. It's impossible to get there from inside. But all five wings have boards and planks lying about and large piles of wood-shavings. I'll drag all the boards and planks together and set fire to them. My pockets are full of all kinds of inflammable materials.

ALVA: But you'll burn up along with it!

HUGENBERG: Of course, unless I'm rescued. But to get into the first court-yard I have to have the jailer on my side, and I need money for that. Not that I mean to bribe him; that would never work. I'd have to loan him some money to send his three children to the country. And then at four in the morning, when prisoners from respectable families are released, I'd slip through the door. He'll lock up behind me. He'll ask me what I want. I'll ask him to let me out again in the morning. And before daylight I'll have made it into the attic.

ALVA: How did you escape the reformatory?

HUGENBERG: Through the window. I'll need two hundred Marks for the jailer to send his children to the country.

RODRIGO (*stepping from behind the portieres*): Will the Baron have his coffee in the music room or on the veranda?

HUGENBERG: Where did *he* come from?! — From the same door! — He jumped through the same door!

ALVA: I've taken him into my service. He's quite dependable.

HUGENBERG (*grasping his head*): You stupid idiot! — You stupid idiot!

RODRIGO: Yes, of course, we met here before. But if I see

you again these next two weeks, I'll beat your brains into a stew.

ALVA: Will you be quiet!

HUGENBERG: What a stupid idiot I am!

RODRIGO: Now what is all this about inflammable materials? — Don't you know she died three weeks ago?

HUGENBERG: Did they cut off her head?

RODRIGO: No — she died of cholera.

HUGENBERG: I don't believe it.

RODRIGO: What do you know about it? — Here, read this — look. (*Taking out a newspaper and pointing to a story in it.*) "The murderess of Doctor Schoen. . ." (*Gives* HUGENBERG *the paper.*)

HUGENBERG (*reading*): "The murderess of Doctor Schoen has quite mysteriously fallen ill of cholera in prison." — Nothing here about her dying.

RODRIGO: What else could she have done? She was buried in the churchyard three weeks ago. The rear left-hand corner behind the rubbish heap, where the little crosses without names are located. She's under the first one. You'll recognize the spot because no grass has grown there. Hang a tin cross on it and then see you get back to your nursery school, or I'll hand you over to the police. I happen to know the female who used you to sweeten her leisure hours.

HUGENBERG (*to* ALVA): Is she really dead?

ALVA: Thank God, yes! — But I must ask you not to take up any more of my time. My doctor forbids me to have visitors.

HUGENBERG: I have so little future now I'd gladly have given her the last sweetness of my life. Damn! I'm done for now one way or other.

RODRIGO: You come too near me or the Doctor here, or my good friend Schigolch, and I'll have you arrested for intended arson. You need two years' hard labor to teach you the proper place for your fingers. — Now get out!

HUGENBERG: What a stupid idiot I am!

RODRIGO: Out! (*Throws* HUGENBERG *out the door. Then comes downstage.*) I'm surprised you didn't offer *him* some money too!

ALVA: You will spare me your obscenities. That boy has more worth in his little finger than all of you put together.

RODRIGO: I've had about enough of that Geschwitz woman. If my fiancee is to become a limited liability corporation, then I'll gladly resign my position. I expect to make a magnificent trapeze artist out of her, and I'm willing to risk my life for it. But then I'll be master in my own house and I'll decide what cavaliers she's to receive.

ALVA: That boy has what our age lacks. A heroic spirit. Which, of course, will be his undoing. Do you remember how before he was sentenced he jumped from the witness stand and screamed at the judge: "What would you have done at ten if you'd had to run around barefoot at night in cafes?!"

RODRIGO: I wish I could have landed him one on the snout! — Thank God there are jails that teach scum like that respect for the law.

ALVA: He could have been the model for my *Ruler of the World*. For twenty years literature has produced nothing but half-men: men unable to beget children and women unable to bear them. It's what's called the "Modern Dilemma."

RODRIGO: I've ordered a two-inch-thick hippopotamus-hide whip. If that doesn't have any effect on her then I'm dumber than I thought. Loving or whipping — it's all one to a woman. Amuse them a bit and they'll stay firm and fresh. This one's twenty years old, been married three times, satisfied incredible numbers of lovers, and is finally showing some evidence of a heart. But a man must be as evil as sin or she has no respect for him. If a man looks as if he'd been spat out by the dog-catcher on the street, he needn't fear even a prince's competition where women like her are concerned. I'll rent a garage fifty feet high, and train her in it. And from the moment she makes her first dive without breaking her neck, I'll slip into my black frock coat and never lift a finger again. If a wife's properly trained, she can support a husband for half as much as the other way around. As long as her husband sees to the mental work, of course, and doesn't let the family go down the drain.

ALVA: I've learned to control mankind and drive it like a well-broken-in four-in-hand — but I can't get that boy out of my mind. I could have taken private lessons in cynicism from him.

RODRIGO: She can comfortably paper her hide with thousand-

Mark bills if she likes. I'll extract her wages from her managers with a centrifugal pump. I know their kind. Let them *not* need a performer, and you can lick their boots; but the minute they *need* one they'll personally cut her down from the gallows with the most engaging compliments.

ALVA: Considering my financial situation, I have nothing to fear in this world but death. But in the world of sensation I'm the neediest of beggars. Yet I can't raise the moral courage necessary to exchange my established ways for the excitements of a life of wild adventure.

RODRIGO: She sent Papa Schigolch and me out to hunt up some strong cure for insomnia for her. We each got a twenty-Mark bill for travel expenses. And then we saw the boy in the Night Light Cafe. He sat there like a criminal on the prisoner's bench. Schigolch sniffed at him from all sides and said: "He's still a virgin."

(*Dragging footsteps are heard in the gallery.*)

RODRIGO: There she is! — The future most magnificent trapeze artist of our time!

(*The curtain at the head of the stairs parts and* LULU, *in a black dress, and leaning on* SCHIGOLCH'S *arm, slowly drags herself down the stairs.*)

SCHIGOLCH: Gitty-up there, old hossey! We still have to cross the border today.

RODRIGO (*staring at* LULU *with a stupid expression*): What in the name of God —?!

LULU (*speaks quite cheerfully to the end of the act*): Careful. You're squeezing my arm.

RODRIGO: How did you have the nerve to break out of prison with a face like that!

SCHIGOLCH: Shut up!

RODRIGO: I'm going for the police! I'll turn you in! Imagine this scarecrow showing herself in tights! Why, the padding alone would cost two months' pay! — You're the biggest fake who ever spent a night in the can.

ALVA: You will kindly not insult the lady.

RODRIGO: You call that an insult? — To think I've brought my belly to this state for that bag of gnarled bones! I can't work like this. I'd be a clown if all I had to do was only lift a broomstick. But may I be struck dead on the spot if I don't rake myself in a salary of ten thousand Marks a year from fraud and swindling! I can assure you of that. Bon voyage! I'm going for the police. (*He goes off.*)

SCHIGOLCH: Well, go then!

LULU: He won't do anything.

SCHIGOLCH: At least we're rid of him. — Now, some black coffee for the young lady.

ALVA: (*at the table downstage left*): Here it is: we can help ourselves.

SCHIGOLCH: I still have to get the sleeping-car tickets.

LULU (*brightly*): Freedom! My God!

SCHIGOLCH: I'll pick you up in half an hour. We'll celebrate our departure at the station restaurant. I'll order a supper that'll last us till tomorrow morning. — Good morning, Doctor!

ALVA: Good evening!

SCHIGOLCH: Sleep tight! — Thanks, I know every door knob in this place. Goodbye! Enjoy yourself! — (*Goes off through the center door.*)

LULU: I haven't seen a room for a year and a half — curtains and chairs and pictures. . .

ALVA: Don't you want the coffee?

LULU: I've drunk quite enough coffee these last few days. Isn't there any whisky?

ALVA: Elixir de Spa?

LULU: That brings back old times. (*Looks around the room as* ALVA *pours two glasses.*) What's happened to my picture?

ALVA: I've hung it in my room so no one will see it.

LULU: Go and get it for me.

ALVA: Still the old vanity? — Despite the prison?

LULU: It's a terrible thing not seeing yourself for months at a time. Then one day I got a grand new dustpan. At seven in the morning when I swept the floor, I used the back of it for a mirror. The tin didn't flatter me, of course, but I enjoyed it. — Get the picture for me from your room. Shall I come with you?

ALVA: Certainly not — you must take care of yourself.

LULU: I've taken care of myself long enough.

(ALVA *goes out for the picture through the door at left.*)

LULU (*alone*): He has a weak heart. Imagine tormenting himself for fourteen months with that illusion. . . His kisses are tinged with the fear of death, and his knees shake like a frozen tramp's. My God! —— If only I hadn't shot his father in this room.

(ALVA *returns with* LULU's *picture as Pierrot.*)

ALVA: It's quite dusty. I leaned it face to the wall against the fireplace.

LULU: You haven't looked at it since I left?

ALVA: I had the sale of the newspaper to attend to. Countess Geschwitz would have liked hanging it in her house, but she knew the police might search it at any time. (*He lifts the picture onto the easel.*)

LULU (*happily*): Now the poor monster's learning the joys of free government housing first hand.

ALVA: I still don't understand how all this hangs together.

LULU: Countess Geschwitz arranged it all very well; I admire her inventiveness. There must have been a terrible cholera epidemic in Hamburg this summer. She based her plan for my escape on it. She took a course in nursing here, and when she had earned the necessary documents she went to Hamburg to nurse the cholera patients. The first chance that came about, she dressed herself in the underclothes of a patient who had just died, and which should have been burned. That same morning she traveled here and visited me in jail. Then while the guard was out, we exchanged underclothes in my cell.

ALVA: So that's how you both fell ill of cholera on the same day!

LULU: Of course. Exactly. — Geschwitz was immediately taken from her house to the isolation ward of the hospital. They didn't know what else to do with me either. So we lay there in one room in the isolation ward behind the hospital. From the first, Geschwitz did everything to make our faces resemble each other as much as possible. The day before yesterday she was released as having been cured.

Just now she came back to say she'd forgotten her watch. I put on her clothes, and she slipped into my prison smock, and then I left. (*Pleased.*) So now she's lying there as the murderess of Doctor Schoen.

ALVA: Outwardly you still agree with the picture, as much as can be expected.

LULU: My face is thinner, but otherwise I've lost nothing. Except that in prison you become terribly nervous.

ALVA: You looked ill when you came in just now.

LULU: I had to, to get that clown off our necks.—But what have you been doing these eighteen months?

ALVA: I had a *succès d'estime* in a literary society with a play I wrote about you.

LULU: Who's your sweetheart now?

ALVA: An actress I've rented a house for in Karlstrasse.

LULU: Does she love you?

ALVA: How should I know? I haven't seen her in six weeks.

LULU: Can you bear that?

ALVA: That's something you'll never understand. There's a close interplay between my sensuality and my creative impulses, so that where you're concerned I have the choice of either exploiting you artistically or of loving you.

LULU (*as though telling a fairy tale*): Every other night I used to dream I'd fallen into the hands of a sex-murderer. Come on, give me a kiss.

ALVA: Your eyes shimmer like the surface of a deep pool into which a stone has been thrown.

LULU: Come on.

ALVA (*kisses her*): Your lips have become very thin.

LULU: Come on! (*She pushes him into a chair and sits on his knee.*) Do I repulse you? — In jail we all got a lukewarm bath once a month. No sooner were we in the water than the guards searched our pockets. (*She kisses him passionately.*)

ALVA: Oh, oh!

LULU: Are you afraid that when I'm gone you won't be able to write any more poems about me?

ALVA: — On the contrary — I'll write a dithyramb to your beauty.

Lulu: The only thing I don't like are these terrible shoes I'm wearing.

Alva: They don't detract from your charm. Let's be grateful for the favor of this moment.

Lulu: I'm not in the mood for that today. — Do you remember the costume-ball, when I dressed as a pageboy? And the tipsy women who kept running after me? Countess Geschwitz grovelled at my feet and begged me to step on her face with my cloth shoe.

Alva: My darling!

Lulu (*in a tone of voice with which one calms a restless child*): Shh — I shot your father.

Alva: I don't love you any the less for that. Kiss me!

Lulu: Lean back your head. (*Kisses him with deliberation.*)

Alva: You know exactly how to keep my passion in check. Even your breathing is chaste. And yet, if it weren't for your two big dark childish eyes, I'd take you for the most cunning whore who ever brought a man to destruction.

Lulu (*cheerfully*): I wish to God I were. Won't you cross the border with us today? We can see each other then as often as we like and enjoy ourselves more than we can now.

Alva: Your body feels like a symphony through your dress. These slender ankles, this capriccio; and the powerful andante of voluptuousness. — How peacefully these two slender rivals lie pressed together, knowing, knowing that neither is the other's equal in beauty — until their capricious mistress wakens and the two lovers part like hostile poles. I'll sing your praises till your senses reel!

Lulu (*gaily*): Meanwhile I'll busy my hands in your hair. (*She does so.*) But we might be disturbed here.

Alva: You've robbed me of my reason!

Lulu: Aren't you coming with us today?

Alva: But the old man's going with you.

Lulu: We won't be seeing him again. — Isn't that the sofa your father bled to death on?

Alva: Be still. . . be still. . .

ACT TWO

A spacious room in white stucco with wide folding-doors in each of the two side walls. Between the doors in the left wall, a white marble-topped rococo console. Above it hangs the picture of LULU *as Pierrot set into the wall in a narrow gold frame. In the middle of the room, a fragile, brightly upholstered Louis XV sofa. Wide, brightly upholstered chairs with thin legs and fragile armrests. Downstage right a small table; left, an entrance way. The most downstage door leads into the dining room. The center door is open and discloses a wide baccarata table, surrounded by upholstered Turkish chairs.* ALVA SCHOEN, RODRIGO QUAST, MARQUIS CASTI-PIANI, PUNTSCHU *the banker,* HEILMANN *the journalist,* LULU, COUNTESS GESCHWITZ, MAGELONE, KADIDJA, BIANETTA, *and* LUDMILLA STEINHERZ *move about the room in animated conversation. The men are in evening dress.* — LULU *wears a white Directoire gown with great sleeves and white lace falling from the waist to feet; her arms are in white kid gloves, her hair done high on her head with a small tuft of white feathers.* — COUNTESS GESCHWITZ *is dressed in a light blue fur-trimmed Hussar's jacket with silver braid, a white bow-tie, tight stand-up collar, and stiff cuffs with enormous ivory links.* — MAGELONE *is in a bright rainbow colored shot silk dress with very wide arms, long narrow waist, and three ruffles of spiral rose colored ribbons with a bouquet of violets. Her hair is parted in the middle, falling deeply over her temples, and curled at the sides. On her forehead she wears a mother-of-pearl ornament, held there by a delicate chain drawn through her hair.* KADIDJA, *her twelve year old daughter, wears bright green satin boots which reveal the tops of her white stockings. Her bodice is of white lace, with bright green narrow sleeves and pearl gray kid gloves. Her black hair is loose; on it she wears a large bright green lace hat with a white feather. —* BIANETTA *is in a dark green velvet dress, with a wide collar sewn with pearls, bloused sleeves, full skirt without a waist, and with a hem embroidered with imitation topazes set in silver. —* LUDMILLA STEINHERZ *is in a gaudy red and white striped summer resort dress.*

RODRIGO (*a full glass in his hand*): Ladies and gentlemen — I beg your pardon — would you kindly be quiet — I drink — with your permission I drink — for this is the birthday celebration of our beloved hostess — (*taking* LULU *by the arm*) — the Countess Adelaide d'Oubra. — Damnation! — And therefore I drink —— and so on and so forth, ladies!

(*They all surround* LULU *and clink glasses with her.*)

ALVA (*shaking* RODRIGO'S *hand*): Congratulations.

RODRIGO: I'm sweating like a pig.

ALVA (*to* LULU): Let's see if everything's in order in the gaming-room.

(*They both go off into the gaming-room.*)

BIANETTA (*to* RODRIGO): Someone just told me, sir, that you're the strongest man in the world.

RODRIGO: That's correct, miss. May I place my strength at your disposal?

MAGELONE: Actually I prefer sharp-shooters. Three months ago a sharp-shooter came to the casino, and every time he went bang I went like this. (*She wriggles her hips.*)

CASTI-PIANI (*speaks in a bored, enervated tone throughout the act; to* MAGELONE): Tell me, my dear, how is it we're seeing your charming little daughter for the first time tonight?

MAGELONE: Do you really think her charming? — She's still in the convent. She must be back to school next Monday.

KADIDJA: What did you say, Mummy?

MAGELONE: I was just telling this gentleman you made the highest grade in geometry last week.

HEILMANN: What beautiful hair she has.

CASTI-PIANI: Just look at her feet! And the way she walks!

PUNTSCHU: My God, that's real breeding!

MAGELONE (*smiling*): Have pity on her, gentlemen; she's only a child.

PUNTSCHU (*to* MAGELONE): That wouldn't bother me in the least. — (*To* HEILMANN.) I'd give ten years of my life to initiate this little lady into the rites of our secret cult.

MAGELONE: Not for a million! No one's ruining this child's youth, as someone did mine.

CASTI-PIANI: Confessions of a lonely soul. (*To* MAGELONE.) Would you consent to a set of genuine diamonds?

MAGELONE: Don't brag! I'm as likely to get diamonds from you as my daughter is. And you know that as well as I.

(KADIDJA *goes into the gaming-room.*)

GESCHWITZ: Aren't we playing this evening?

LUDMILLA STEINHERZ: Certainly, Countess. I've been counting on it.

BIANETTA: Then let's take our places at once. The men will follow us shortly.

GESCHWITZ: Would you excuse me for a second. I have something to say to my friends.

CASTI-PIANI (*offering* BIANETTA *his arm*): May I have the honor of being your partner? You have a very lucky hand.

LUDMILLA STEINHERZ: You may give me your other arm and then lead us all into the gaming-hall.

(CASTI-PIANI *goes into the gaming-room with the two women.*)

MAGELONE: Tell me, Mr. Puntschu, do you have any more Jungfrau shares for me?

PUNTSCHU: Jungfrau shares? (*To* HEILMANN.) The lady means shares in the cable-railway up the Jungfrau peak. The Jungfrau is a mountain up which they intend to build a cable railway. (*To* MAGELONE.) I say this only to avoid confusion, you understand. That were an easy thing in so select a gathering. — The fact is, I have approximately four thousand more shares of Jungfrau stock, but I prefer to keep them for myself. The opportunity of making oneself a small fortune may not come soon again.

HEILMANN: So far I've only a single share of this Jungfrau stock. I'd like some more myself.

PUNTSCHU: I'll do what I can, Mr. Heilmann. But I must warn you, you'll be paying stiff prices.

MAGELONE: My fortune-teller said to be on the lookout for them, so I'd be prepared. My entire savings are in Jungfrau stock. If it falls through, Mr. Puntschu, I'll scratch your eyes out.

PUNTSCHU: I know perfectly well what I'm about, my dear.

ALVA (*reentering from the gaming-room; to* MAGELONE): I assure you, your fears are totally unfounded. I paid very dearly for my shares, and I've never regretted it for a moment. They're on a steady daily rise. There's never been anything like it.

MAGELONE: So much the better, then, if you're right. (*Taking* PUNTSCHU'S *arm.*) Come! Let's try our hand at baccarat.

(MAGELONE, PUNTSCHU, ALVA, *and* HEILMANN *go into the gaming-room.* — RODRIGO *and* COUNTESS GESCHWITZ *stay behind.*)

RODRIGO (*scribbles something on a piece of paper and folds it; noticing* GESCHWITZ): My dear Countess. . . (*As* GESCHWITZ *starts.*) Do I look as dangerous as all that? (*To himself.*) I must deliver some sort of bon-mot. (*Aloud.*) May I make so bold as to. . . ?

GESCHWITZ: Go to hell!

CASTI-PIANI (*leading* LULU *into the hall*): If you will allow me a word or two. . .

LULU (*while* RODRIGO *furtively passes her the piece of paper*): As many as you like. . .

RODRIGO: With your permission I will excuse myself. (*He goes off into the gaming-room.*)

CASTI-PIANI (*to* GESCHWITZ): Leave us alone.

LULU (*to* CASTI-PIANI): Have I hurt you again in some way?

CASTI-PIANI (*when* GESCHWITZ *doesn't budge*): Are you deaf?

(*Sighing deeply,* GESCHWITZ *goes into the gaming-room.*)

LULU: Why not just come out and tell me how much you want?

CASTI-PIANI: You can no longer help me with money.

LULU: What makes you think we're out of money?

CASTI-PIANI: You handed over your last penny to me yesterday.

LULU: If you're so certain, then it must be true.

CASTI-PIANI: You and this writer of yours are left without a cent.

LULU: Then why all the talk? If you want me for yourself, you needn't threaten me first with execution.

CASTI-PIANI: I know that. But I've told you any number of times now that you're not my type. I haven't fleeced you because you love me; rather, I loved you so as to be *able* to fleece you. Bianetta's more attractive to me than you ever were. You exhibit the choicest delicacies, and then when one has frittered away his time over them, he ends up hungrier than before. You've loved too long, even by prevailing standards. All you do for a healthy young man is ruin his nervous system. But you're all the more suited for the position I've picked out for you.

LULU: You're mad! — Did I ask you to find me a job?

CASTI-PIANI: I told you I'm an employment agent.

LULU: You said you were a police spy.

CASTI-PIANI: You don't make a living that way. I began as an employment agent, until I slipped up over a preacher's daughter that I'd given a job in Valparaiso. In her childish dreams the sweet little thing had imagined life more intoxicating than it actually is, and complained about it to her mother. Whereupon I was thrown in jail. By virtue of my excellent character I quickly won over the confidence of the police. They sent me here with a monthly allowance of one hundred and fifty Marks. They were tripling our contingent here because of these endless bombings. But who can live on one hundred and fifty Marks a month? — My colleagues let themselves be kept by women. Naturally it was more expedient for me to resume my former calling; and of the countless number of adventuresses who congregate here from the best families in the world,

I've sent many a young creature hungry for life to the place of her natural vocation.

LULU (*decisively*): I wouldn't be much good at that.

CASTI-PIANI: Your opinions on the subject don't interest me in the least. The state prosecutor's office will pay one thousand Marks to anyone who delivers to them the murderess of Doctor Ludwig Schoen. All I need do is whistle for the policeman down on the corner and I'll have earned a thousand Marks. On the other hand, the Oikonomopulos Establishment in Cairo is offering sixty pounds for you — twelve hundred Marks — two hundred Marks more than the prosecutor's office. And besides, I'm still enough of a philanthropist to help my mistresses to happiness, rather than plunge them into misfortune.

LULU (*as above*): A woman like myself could never be happy in a house like that. It might have pleased me when I was fifteen. At the time I doubted I'd ever be happy. I bought a revolver; and at night ran barefoot across the bridge to shoot myself in the snow. Then I had the good fortune of lying in the hospital for three months without ever seeing a man. It was then my eyes were opened and I saw myself as I really was. Night after night I dreamt of the man I was made for and who was made for me. Then when I was set loose again upon men, I was no longer a silly goose. Ever since, I've been able to tell in the dead of night and at a hundred paces whether a man and I are made for each other. And if I find I've sinned against my judgment, the next day I feel soiled both inside and out, and it takes weeks to overcome my loathing for myself. And here you are, thinking I'll throw myself at every no-good so-and-so.

CASTI-PIANI: No-good so-and-sos don't frequent Oikonomopulos' in Cairo. His clientele consists of Scottish lords, Russian dignitaries, Indian rulers and our own jolly Rhineland big-business industrialists. All you need is to speak French. But with your excellent talent for languages you'll even pick up enough English for your needs. And you'll live in a royally furnished apartment with a view onto the minarets of El-Azhar mosque, and walk all day long on Persian carpets as thick as your fists. In the evening you'll dress in fabulous Parisian gowns, drink as much champagne as your customers can buy you; and finally, up to a certain degree at least, you'll be your own mistress. If the man doesn't please you, you'll simply show him no feelings. You'll allow him to leave his visiting card, of course — but that's the end of it. If the ladies didn't train themselves to it, the whole business would be impossible, because after four weeks everyone would go straight to the devil.

LULU (*with a trembling voice*): I think you've developed a loose screw somewhere since yesterday. Do you mean Egyptians will pay five hundred marks for someone they've never seen?

CASTI-PIANI: I took the liberty of sending pictures of you.

LULU: You sent him the pictures *I* gave you?

CASTI-PIANI: As you can see, he knows how to value them better than I. Once you're there, he'll probably hang up over the door that picture of you as Eve in front of the mirror. Just remember one other thing: you're safer from your pursuers in Cairo than if you'd crept into a Canadian wilderness. They're not likely to transfer an Egyptian courtesan to a German prison — first, because of the expense, and second, for fear of coming too near Eternal Justice.

LULU (*proudly with a clear voice*): I don't give a damn about your Eternal Justice! I will not be locked up in any such place of amusement.

CASTI-PIANI: Shall I whistle for the policeman?

LULU (*amazed*): If you need money, why not just ask me for twelve hundred Marks?

CASTI-PIANI: I don't need money. — And I haven't asked you because you don't have any.

LULU: We still have thirty thousand Marks.

CASTI-PIANI: In Jungfrau stocks. I never get involved in stocks. The state prosecutor pays in German National Currency, and Oikonomopulos in English gold. You could be on board early tomorrow. The voyage won't take more than five days. Two weeks at most and you'll be safe. You're nearer jail here than anywhere else. As a member of the secret police, I can't understand how you've lived here unmolested for a whole year. Considering your heavy consumption of men, it's not unlikely one of my colleagues will make the same happy discovery as I — sniffing out the trail of your past history. I can wash my hands of you then, and you can spend the rest of your years of enjoyment in prison. I suggest you decide quickly. The train leaves at half-past twelve. If we haven't struck a bargain by eleven, I'll call the policeman. On the other hand, if we do reach an agreement, I'll pack you into a carriage just as you are, drive you to the station, and take you on shipboard tomorrow evening.

LULU: You can't be serious.

CASTI-PIANI: I'm concerned only for your physical safety.

Lulu: I'll go to America with you, to China; but I will no
let myself be sold. That's worse than prison.

Casti-piani: Here — read this effusion! (*He pulls a lette from his pocket.*) I'll read it to you. Here's the postmark "Cairo," just so you don't think I deal in forged documents. The girl was born in Berlin, married two years and to a man whom you might well have envied her — a former colleague of mine. He now travels for some Hamburg colonial enterprise or other.

Lulu (*gaily*): I suppose he *visits* his wife occasionally?

Casti-piani: Quite possibly. But listen to the impulsive way she expresses herself. I think no more highly of my traffic in young girls than the next best judge; but a cry of such joy gives me momentary moral satisfaction. I'm proud to earn my living by scattering happiness with full hands (*He reads.*) "My dear Mr. Meyer" — that's my white-slave trader's name — "When you get to Berlin, you must go at once to the conservatory on Potsdamer Strasse and ask for Gusti von Rosenkron — the most beautiful woman I have ever seen: enchanting hands and feet, a naturally small waist, straight back, full body, large eyes, and short nose — exactly as you like them. I've already written her. She has no future as a singer. Her mother is destitute. Unfortunately she's already twenty-five, but wasting away for love She can't marry because she has no dowry. I've spoken with madame — they would gladly take on another German as long as she is well educated and musical. The Italians and French can't compete with us because of too little culture. If you should happen to see Fritz. . ." — Fritz is her husband; of course he's getting a divorce — ". . .tell him it was all a dull bore. He knew no better than I. . ." Now for the more exact details. . .

Lulu (*goaded*): I can't sell the only thing I've ever owned!

Casti-piani: You will let me continue.

Lulu (*as above*): I'll give you our entire fortune this evening.

Casti-piani: Good God! I told you you have no money! Unless we leave this house by eleven you and your whole pack will be removed to Germany, tomorrow, with a police escort.

Lulu: You *can't* turn me over to them!

Casti-piani: Don't think this is the worst I've ever done. Now, just in case we do leave tonight, I must have a quick word with Bianetta. (*He goes off into the gaming-room, leaving the door open behind him.*)

(LULU *stares in front of her, while mechanically crumpling the note given her by* RODRIGO, *which she has held in her fingers throughout the conversation.* ALVA *rises from behind the gaming-table, some script in his hand, and enters the salon.*)

ALVA (*to* LULU): Brilliant! It's going brilliantly! Geschwitz has just staked her last cent. Puntschu has just promised me two more Jungfrau shares. And Steinherz is making her small profit. (*He goes off downstage right.*)

LULU (*alone*): I? In a brothel? —— (*She reads the note in her hand and begins laughing as though she were mad.*)

ALVA (*reenters downstage right, holding a cashbox*): Aren't you going to play with us?

LULU: Of course, of course. Why not.

ALVA: Incidentally, I read in today's *Berliner Tageblatt* that Alfred Hugenberg threw himself over a balcony in prison.

LULU: You mean *he's* in jail too?

ALVA: It's more of a house of preventive custody. (*He goes off into the gaming-room.*)

(LULU *is about to follow him, but* COUNTESS GESCHWITZ *meets her in the doorway.*)

GESCHWITZ: Are you leaving because of me?

LULU (*resolutely*): Certainly not. But when you come in, I *do* leave.

GESCHWITZ: You've defrauded me of all of my worldly goods. The least you might do is be outwardly polite to me.

LULU (*as above*): I'm as polite with you as with any other woman.

GESCHWITZ: Have you forgotten the time we lay in the hospital together? And with what passionate endearments you seduced me into taking your place?

LULU: Why else did you give me cholera? What I swore during the trial was quite different from what I had to promise you. I shudder that it should ever become a fact.

GESCHWITZ: Then you deliberately deceived me?

LULU (*gaily*): Deceived? About what? Your physical charms have found so enthusiastic an admirer here I wonder whether I won't have to take up teaching piano again for a living. No seventeen year old girl could drive a man madder with love than you, a pervert, have this poor fellow with your bitchiness!

GESCHWITZ: Who? I don't understand.

LULU (*gaily*): Your acrobat, Rodrigo Quast. He's an athlete; he balances two fully-saddled horses on his chest. What more can a woman ask for? He just told me unless you take pity on him, he'll drown himself — tonight.

GESCHWITZ: I don't envy you your skill in tormenting the victims fate sacrifices to you. I don't in the least envy you. My own misery has never wrung from me the pity I feel for you. I feel free as a god when I think of the creatures who have *you* enslaved.

LULU: What do you mean?

GESCHWITZ: Casti-Piani, whose degenerate baseness is written on his forehead in letters of fire.

LULU: Shut up! Say anything bad about that boy and I'll kick you in the stomach! He loves me with an honesty that makes your most extravagant sacrifices seem a beggary. His self-denial makes me see how loathsome you really are. You weren't finished in your mother's womb, and now you're neither man nor woman. You aren't human as the rest of us. There wasn't enough to make a man of you, and you have too many brains for a woman. That's why you're mad. Why not take a fancy to Miss Bianetta? She's available to anyone for a price. Put a gold coin in her hand and she's yours.

(BIANETTA, MAGELONE, LUDMILLA STEINHERZ, RODRIGO, CASTI-PIANI, PUNTSCHU, HEILMANN, *and* ALVA *enter the salon from the gaming-room.*)

LULU: Good God, what's happened?

PUNTSCHU: Nothing. We're thirsty, that's all.

MAGELONE: We've all been winning; it's unbelievable.

BIANETTA: I must have won a fortune.

LUDMILLA STEINHERZ: You mustn't boast of it, child. It's unlucky.

MAGELONE: But the bank has won, too. How is that possible?

ALVA: Where's all the money coming from?

CASTI-PIANI: Better not to ask. Let's be satisfied that we needn't spare on the champagne.

HEILMANN: After this, I can buy a dinner in a respectable restaurant.

ALVA: To the buffet, ladies! To the buffet!

(*The entire assembly retires to the dining-room.— LULU is detained by RODRIGO.*)

RODRIGO: One moment, my dear.—Did you read my love-note?

LULU: Threaten me with the police as much as you like. I no longer dispose of money in twenty-thousand-Mark sums. I don't have it.

RODRIGO: Don't lie to me, you whore. You've got forty thousand left in Jungfrau stocks. Your so-called husband's just been bragging about it.

LULU: Then blackmail *him*. I don't care what he does with his money.

RODRIGO: You're very kind. I'd need two days to get through to him. And when he finally understands, he kills you with explanations. Meanwhile my fiancee writes me that it's all over and I can hang a barrel-organ around my neck.

LULU: Have you gotten yourself engaged?

RODRIGO: Was I supposed to get your permission first? Did you thank me for freeing you from prison at the cost of my health?—You've abandoned me. I might have had to become a porter if this girl hadn't taken me on. At my first performance here a velvet armchair was thrown at me. This country has grown too decadent to value genuine feats of strength. If I'd been a boxing kangaroo, I'd have been interviewed and photographed for all the papers. Thank God I'd already made my Celestine's acquaintance. She has twenty years' savings deposited at the National Bank. Besides that, she loves me for myself. She's interested in more than just obscenities, unlike you. She has three children by an American bishop; and all of them show the greatest promise. The day after tomorrow we'll be married by the registrar.

LULU: You have my blessings.

RODRIGO: The hell with your blessings! I told her I had twenty thousand in stocks in the bank.

LULU (*amused*): She loves him for himself!

RODRIGO: She admires my sensitivity, not my strength, like you and all the others. But that's all over now. First they tear the clothes off your back, and then they wallow around with the chambermaid. I'd rather be dead than submit myself to such amusements again.

LULU: Then why are you pestering poor Countess Geschwitz with your proposals?

RODRIGO: Because she's a noblewoman. I'm a man of the world; I know more about civilized conversations than any of you.—But now I'm sick of it all. Do I get the money by tomorrow evening, or not?

LULU: I don't have any money.

RODRIGO: How stupid do you think I am? Do your duty by him once and he'll give you his last cent. You lured the poor boy here. It's all he can do now to scrape up a job worthy of him.

LULU: It's not your business if he squanders his money on women or at gaming-tables!

RODRIGO: You're determined to waste his father's last cent on this rabble of yours! You'll make four people happy if you're not too exact and sacrifice yourself to a worthy cause. Why is everything always Casti-Piani? I

LULU (*gaily*): Shall I have him light you down the stairs?

RODRIGO: Whatever you say, Countess. Unless I have the twenty thousand Marks by tomorrow evening, the information I give the police will bring this court of yours to a very sudden halt. — Goodbye.

(HEILMANN *the journalist enters out of breath from upstage right.*)

LULU: Are you looking for Miss Magelone? — She's not here.

HEILMANN: No, I'm looking for something else.

RODRIGO (*pointing to the door opposite*): The second door on the left, sir.

LULU (*to* RODRIGO): Did your fiancee teach you that?

HEILMANN (*bumping into* PUNTSCHU *the banker in the doorway*): Excuse me, my angel.

PUNTSCHU: Oh, it's you! Miss Magelone's waiting for you in the elevator.

HEILMANN: Would you ride up with her please. I'll be right back. (*He hurries off through the main entrance.*)

(LULU *goes into the dining-room;* RODRIGO *follows her.*)

PUNTSCHU (*alone*): The heat in here is unbearable. —— If I don't cut off yours, you'll cut off mine. —— If I don't rent out my John Thomas, I'll have to rely on my brains. — My brains don't get wrinkles, they don't get indisposed, and they don't need to bathe in Eau de Cologne.

(BOB, *a fifteen-year-old groom in red jacket, tight leather breeches, and shining top boots, brings in a telegram.*)

BOB: Mr. Puntschu the banker!

PUNTSCHU (*breaks open the telegram and mumbles*): "Jungfrau cable-railway stocks fallen to. . ." — well, well, that's the way of the world. (*To* BOB.) Wait. (*Gives him a tip.*) Tell me — what's your name?

BOB: My real name is Freddy but everyone calls me Bob because it's the style now.

PUNTSCHU: How old are you?

BOB: Fifteen.

KADIDJA (*enters hesitantly from the gaming-room*): Excuse me, could you tell me if Mama is here?

PUNTSCHU: No, child. — (*To himself.*) My God, she's well-bred!

KADIDJA: I've been looking all over for her; I can't find her anywhere.

PUNTSCHU: Your Mama will turn up again, just as sure as my name is Puntschu. —— (*Looking at* BOB.) My goodness, those knee breeches you're wearing! —— Merciful Heavens! It makes a person feel absolutely uncanny! (*Goes off upstage right.*)

KADIDJA (*to* BOB): Have you seen my Mama?

BOB: No — but why don't you just come with me?

KADIDJA: Where is she?

BOB: She rode up in the elevator. Come on.

KADIDJA: No, no, I don't want to ride up!

BOB: We can hide upstairs in the corridor.

KADIDJA: No, no — I won't, or I'll get scolded!

(MAGELONE *rushes through the main entrance, very excitedly, and seizes* KADIDJA.)

MAGELONE: Oh, so there you are, you common little creature!

KADIDJA: Oh, Mama, Mama, I looked everywhere for you!

MAGELONE: Looked for me? ! Did I tell you to look for me? ! What have you been up to with this man?

(HEILMANN, ALVA, LUDMILLA STEINHERZ, PUNTSCHU, COUNTESS GESCHWITZ, *and* LULU *enter from the dining-room.* BOB *has gone out.*)

MAGELONE (*to* KADIDJA): — Will you stop screaming in front of all these people! Listen to me now!

(*They all surround* KADIDJA.)

LULU: You're crying, my sweet! Won't you tell me why?

PUNTSCHU: God knows, she's *really* been crying. Has anyone hurt you, my little goddess?

LUDMILLA STEINHERZ (*kneels in front of* KADIDJA *and takes her in her arms*): Come, tell me, little angel, what's so bad. Would you like some cake? Would you like some chocolate?

MAGELONE: It's her nerves. She's developing them much too soon. The best thing is just to ignore her.

PUNTSCHU: That sounds just like you. Fine mother you are. The courts will take the child away from you and appoint me her guardian. (*Pats* KADIDJA's *cheek.*) Isn't that right, my little goddess?

GESCHWITZ: I'll be glad when we get back to playing baccarat.

(*The assembly retires to the dining-room.* LULU *is detained at the door by* BOB, *who whispers something to her.*)

LULU: Of course. Let him in.

(BOB *opens the door to the corridor and lets* SCHIGOLCH *in. He is in evening dress, with heel-worn patent leather boots, and shabby opera hat, which he keeps on his head.*)

SCHIGOLCH (*with a glance at* BOB): Where did you get *him?*

LULU: From the circus.

SCHIGOLCH: How much do you pay him?

LULU: Ask him, if you're interested. (*To* BOB.) Close the door.

(BOB *goes into the dining-room and closes the door behind him.*)

SCHIGOLCH (*seating himself*): The fact is, you see, I need some money. I've rented an apartment for my mistress.

LULU: *You've* taken a mistress here, too?

SCHIGOLCH: She's from Frankfurt. In her youth she was the wife of the King of Naples. Every day she assures me she was once very captivating.

LULU (*with apparent outward calm*): Does she need the money badly?

SCHIGOLCH: She wants to furnish her own apartment. And of course sums of that sort mean nothing to you.

LULU (*is suddenly taken with a crying fit and throws herself at* SCHIGOLCH'S *feet*): Dear God in Heaven!

SCHIGOLCH (*patting her*): What is it? — What's the matter?

LULU (*swallows convulsively*): It's too terrible to talk about!

SCHIGOLCH (*pulls her onto his knee and holds her in his arms like a small child*): Hm — you're trying to do too much, my child. — You ought to go to bed now and then with a good novel. — You just go on and cry; cry it all out. — The same thing happened to you before — fifteen years ago. No human being has ever screamed since, the way you screamed then. — At the time, though, you didn't have a tuft of feathers in your hair; nor were you wearing transparent stockings. You had neither shoes nor stockings then.

LULU (*howling*): Take me home with you! Take me home with you tonight! We can find a carriage downstairs.

SCHIGOLCH: Of course I'll take you, of course. — But what's the matter?

LULU: My life depends on it! They're going to turn me over to the police.

SCHIGOLCH: Who? Who's turning you over to the police?

LULU: The acrobat.

SCHIGOLCH (*with absolute calm*): I'll take care of him.

LULU (*imploringly*): Oh, yes, please. You must, you must take care of him. Then you can do whatever you want with me.

SCHIGOLCH: If he comes to see me, he's done for. My window looks out over the river. But — (*shaking his head*) — he won't come.

LULU: What's your number?

SCHIGOLCH: 376, the last house before the Hippodrome.

LULU: I'll send him to you. He'll be there with that idiot who keeps grovelling at my feet. He'll be there this evening. Go on home now so they'll find it comfortable when they get there.

SCHIGOLCH: Just let them come.

LULU: Tomorrow bring me the golden rings he wears in his ears.

SCHIGOLCH: He wears rings in his ears?

LULU: Take them off before you throw him out. He won't notice a thing if he's drunk.

SCHIGOLCH: And then? What then, my child?

LULU: I'll give you the money for your mistress.

SCHIGOLCH: I'd call that a bit stingy.

LULU: And anything else you want. Whatever I have.

SCHIGOLCH: It's been almost ten years since we last knew one another.

LULU: Is that all you want? But you have a mistress.

SCHIGOLCH: My little love from Frankfurt isn't exactly in her prime.

LULU: Then you must swear.

SCHIGOLCH: Haven't I always kept my word to you?

LULU: Swear — swear that you'll take care of him.

SCHIGOLCH: I'll take care of him.

LULU: Swear it to me. Swear it to me.

SCHIGOLCH (*puts his hand on her ankle*): — By everything that's holy. — Tonight, when he comes to see me. —

LULU: By everything that's holy! —— How cool that is.

SCHIGOLCH: No, it makes me hot.

LULU: Go home at once. They'll be there in half an hour. Take a carriage.

SCHIGOLCH: I'm going.

LULU: Hurry! I beg of you! —— My God. . .

SCHIGOLCH: Why are you staring at me like that?

LULU: It's nothing. . .

SCHIGOLCH: Well? — Swallowed your tongue?

LULU: My garter broke.

SCHIGOLCH: So what if it has? Is that all?

LULU: What does it mean?

SCHIGOLCH: What does it mean? I'll tie it for you if you'll hold still.

LULU: It means bad luck.

SCHIGOLCH (*yawning*): Not for you, my child. Don't worry. I'll take care of him. — (Goes off.)

(LULU *places her left foot on the foot-stool, ties her garter, and goes into the gaming-room.* — RODRIGO *is thrust roughly into the salon by* CASTI-PIANI.)

RODRIGO: You could at least treat me with some civility.

CASTI-PIANI (*completely apathetic*): Why should I want to do that? I demand to know what you said to her awhile ago in this room.

RODRIGO: For that you can be a little civil to me.

CASTI-PIANI: Damn you! Answer me. You asked her to ride up with you in the elevator.

RODRIGO: That is a miserable lie.

CASTI-PIANI: She told me so herself. You threatened to turn her over to the police unless she went with you. You want me to shoot you right here?

RODRIGO: You shameless creature. I'd never have thought of such a thing. —And even if I did want her, I wouldn't have to threaten her with prison.

CASTI-PIANI: Thank you. That's all I wanted to know. (*Goes off through the main entrance.*)

RODRIGO: The dog! — I'd like to stick him on the ceiling like a piece of limburger cheese. —— Come back here and I'll wrap your guts around your gullet! —— That'd be even better.

LULU (*reenters from the gaming-room*): What's keeping you? — You're like a needle in a haystack.

RODRIGO: That'll teach him to start things with me!

LULU: Who?

RODRIGO: That Casti-Piani of yours. You damn whore! Why did you tell him I wanted to seduce you?

LULU: You suggested I give myself to my deceased husband's son for twenty-thousand in Jungfrau shares.

RODRIGO: You owe the poor boy some pity. You shot his father from under him in the prime of life. But Casti-Piani will think twice before he runs into me again. I'll lay one in his gut that'll send his insides flying like Roman candles. If he's the best you can find to take my place, I'm sorry I ever had anything to do with you.

LULU: Geschwitz is in a terrible state. She's twisted with pain. She'll drown herself if you keep her waiting any longer.

RODRIGO: What does the old bitch want?

LULU: You. To take her with you.

RODRIGO: Give her my regards, and I hope the water's not too cold.

LULU: She'll loan me twenty thousand Marks to save me. But you must do your part and save *her*. Take her with you tonight, and tomorrow I'll deposit twenty thousand Marks in any bank you like.

RODRIGO: And if I don't take her with me?

LULU: Then call the police. Alva and I are bankrupt.

RODRIGO: I'll be damned!

LULU: You'll make four people happy if you sacrifice yourself to a worthy cause.

RODRIGO: It won't work; I know that right now; I've tried it often enough. Who'd have thought the old bag of bones had so much honor in her. All I ever saw in her was her aristocracy. My behavior was more gentlemanlike than any other German circus artist. If only I'd pinched her calves once.

LULU (*cautiously*): She's still a virgin.

RODRIGO (*sighing*): If God's in His Heaven, you'll pay for your jokes one day. That's for sure.

LULU: She's waiting. What shall I tell her?

RODRIGO: My best regards and that I'm queer.

LULU: I'll see she gets the message.

RODRIGO: Wait! — Are you certain I'll get twenty thousand Marks?

LULU: Ask her.

RODRIGO: Tell her I'm ready. I'll wait for her in the dining-room. I have to see about another barrel of caviar. (*He goes into the dining-room.*)

LULU (*opens the door to the gaming-room and calls brightly*): Martha!

(*At that, the* COUNTESS GESCHWITZ *enters the salon and the door closes behind her.*)

LULU (*pleased*): My love, you have the chance today of saving me from death.

GESCHWITZ: Is it possible?

LULU: By going to a brothel with our acrobat.

GESCHWITZ: But why, my love?

LULU: He says you must be his tonight, or tomorrow morning he'll turn me over to the police.

GESCHWITZ: You know I can never belong to a man; my fate doesn't permit such a thing.

LULU: If you don't satisfy him, that's his problem. Why did he fall in love with you in the first place?

GESCHWITZ: He'll treat me as a beast. He'll avenge himself for his disappointment and beat my head in. I've been through that already. — Can't you spare me this ordeal?

LULU: And what will you get out of it if he turns me over to the police?

GESCHWITZ: I still have enough for us to travel steerage to America. You'd be safe there from your pursuers.

LULU (*pleased and gaily*): I want to stay here. I couldn't be happy in any other city. Tell him you can't live without him. He'll feel flattered then and be as gentle as a lamb. You'll also have to pay the cab-driver. Give him this; it has the address on it. 376 is a sixth-class hotel. They're expecting the two of you this evening.

GESCHWITZ: How can such a monstrosity save your life? — I don't understand. — You've done this to torment me. You've devised the most terrible fate that could befall an outcast like me.

LULU (*cunningly*): Perhaps this will cure you.

GESCHWITZ (*sighing*): Oh, Lulu, if there's such a thing as Eternal Justice, I wouldn't want to be answerable for you! I can't believe that there's no God watching over us. And yet, you're probably right, there's nothing to it. How insignificant I am. How have I provoked God to make horrible for me what is bliss for every other creature?

LULU: You have no right to complain. When you're happy, you're a hundred thousand times happier than the rest of us ordinary mortals.

GESCHWITZ: I'm aware of that too. I envy no one. But I'm still waiting. You've betrayed me so often already.

LULU: I'm yours, my darling, if only you'll keep the acrobat quiet till tomorrow morning. He needs only to have his vanity calmed. You must beg him to take pity on you.

GESCHWITZ: And tomorrow?

LULU: I'll be waiting for you, my love. I won't open my eyes before you come. I'll look at no chambermaid, I'll receive no hairdresser, I won't open my eyes before you come to me.

GESCHWITZ: Then let him come.

LULU: You must throw your arms around his neck, my darling! Do you still have the address?

GESCHWITZ: 376. — Hurry!

LULU (*calls into the dining-room*): Are you ready, my sweet?

RODRIGO (*enters from the dining-room*): You ladies will forgive me for having my mouth full.

GESCHWITZ (*grasps his hand*): I adore you! Take pity on my need!

RODRIGO: *A la bonne heure!* Let us mount the scaffold! (*He offers her his arm and they leave the salon.*)

LULU: Good night, my dears! — (*She accompanies them into the corridor and returns at once with* BOB.) Hurry, Bob, hurry! We must leave at once. You're going with me. But we'll have to change clothes.

BOB (*curt and clearly*): Whatever madame wishes.

LULU (*taking him by the hand*): Madame, Madame! You give me your clothes and you'll put on mine. Come.

(LULU *and* BOB *go off into the dining-room.* — *A commotion arises in the gaming-room; doors are flung open.* PUNTSCHU, HEILMANN, ALVA, BIANETTA, MAGELONE, KADIDJA, *and* LUDMILLA STEINHERZ *enter the salon.*)

HEILMANN (*holding a certificate with a view of an Alpine sunset on it; to* PUNTSCHU): Will you accept this Jungfrau share, sir?!

PUNTSCHU: Without an official quotation?

HEILMANN: Scoundrel! You give me no means of recovering myself, I see!

MAGELONE (*to* BIANETTA): Do you understand any of this?

LUDMILLA STEINHERZ: Puntschu relieved him of all his money and now he's calling off the game.

HEILMANN: He's getting cold feet, the filthy Jew!

PUNTSCHU: What do you mean, calling off the game? What do you mean, getting cold feet? All he has to do is put down cold cash. I'm not in my banking office now. He can offer me his trash tomorrow morning.

HEILMANN: Trash? ! — This share stands at 210!

PUNTSCHU: Yes. Yesterday. Not today. By tomorrow you can paper your walls with it.

ALVA: That's impossible! — That would mean we're bankrupt!

PUNTSCHU: What can I say? *I've* lost *my* entire fortune too! Tomorrow morning I shall be searching for a stable existence for the thirty-sixth time.

MAGELONE (*pressing forward*): I must be dreaming. I must have misunderstood! Did someone say the Jungfrau shares have fallen?

PUNTSCHU: Lower even than you, Madame. — But then you can always use them for curling-papers.

MAGELONE: Merciful Heavens! Ten years' work! (*She faints.*)

KADIDJA: Wake up, Mama, wake up!

BIANETTA: By the way, Mr. Puntschu, where will you have supper this evening, now that you've lost everything?

PUNTSCHU: Wherever you like, my dear young lady. You may take me wherever you wish. But be quick about it. It's growing a bit unpleasant here.

(PUNTSCHU *and* BIANETTA *leave the salon.*)

HEILMANN (*crumples his share into a ball and throws it to the floor*): That's what you get from a pack like this.

LUDMILLA STEINHERZ: Why are *you* speculating on the Jungfrau, too? Why not send an article or two about our little group here to the German police? You might get something out of it.

HEILMANN: I've never done such a thing, but if you care to give me a hand...

LUDMILLA STEINHERZ: We'll go to a restaurant that's open all night. Do you know the *Five-footed Sheep?*

HEILMANN: I'm sorry, I —

LUDMILLA STEINHERZ: Or the *Sucking Calf?* Or the *Smoking Dog?* — They're all right in the neighborhood. We can be alone there. By morning we'll have turned out a priceless little article.

HEILMANN: Don't you ever sleep?

LUDMILLA STEINHERZ: Well, of course! But not at night, certainly.

(HEILMANN *and* LUDMILLA STEINHERZ *leave the salon through the main entrance.*)

ALVA (*bent over* MAGELONE *for some time now, trying to bring her round*): Her hands are ice-cold. — What a magnificent woman! — Someone really ought to undo her waist. She's so tightly laced.

KADIDJA (*without moving*): I'm afraid!

(LULU *enters from the dining-room dressed in a jockey cap, red jacket, white leather breeches, and riding boots, and with a cycling cape around her shoulders.*)

LULU: Do you have any cash, Alva?

ALVA (*looking up*): Have you gone out of your mind?

LULU: The police will be here in two minutes. We've been turned in. You can stay if you like.

ALVA: (*jumping up*): Merciful Heaven!

(LULU *and* ALVA *go off through the main entrance.*)

KADIDJA (*shaking her mother; crying*): Mama! Mama! Please wake up! Everyone's running away!

MAGELONE (*coming to*): My youth gone! — My best days spent! — Oh, what a life!

KADIDJA: But *I'm* still young, Mama! Why can't I earn money, too? — I don't want to go back to the convent. *Please*, Mama, let me stay with you!

MAGELONE: God bless you, my sweet! You don't know what you're saying. — No —I'll look around for an engagement in a variety theatre, and sing to the people of my misfortune with the Jungfrau stocks. They go wild over things like that.

KADIDJA: But you can't sing, Mama.

MAGELONE: Yes, that's true.

KADIDJA: Take me to the variety theatre with you.

MAGELONE: No, it would break my heart. But if that's the way things are ordained, and it can't be otherwise — then there's nothing I can do. —— We'll go to the Olympia tomorrow together.

KADIDJA: Oh, Mama, I'm so happy!

(A POLICE INSPECTOR *in plain clothes enters from the corridor.*)

POLICE INSPECTOR: I arrest you in the name of the law!

CASTI-PIANI (*following him timidly*): What in the name of Heaven do you think you're doing? You've got the wrong one!

ACT THREE

An attic room without windows. Two large panes of glass in the ceiling open outward. Downstage right and left are doors which close badly. By the left proscenium, a tattered mattress. Downstage right, a rickety flower-stand, with a bottle and a smoking oil-lamp on it. In the upstage right corner, an old chaise longue. Beside the center door, a worn cane chair. The sound of rain beating on the roof is heard. A bowl of water stands beneath the skylight. SCHIGOLCH, *in a long, gray overcoat, lies downstage on the mattress.* ALVA SCHOEN *lies on the chaise longue in the corner, wrapped in a rug, the straps of which hang above him on the wall.*

SCHIGOLCH: The rain's beating a tattoo.

ALVA: Very appropriate weather for her debut.—I just dreamt that we were dining together at the Olympia. Bianetta was still there. The table was absolutely soaked with champagne.

SCHIGOLCH: Ah, yes—and I dreamt of a Christmas pudding.

(LULU *enters through the doorway, downstage right. She is barefoot, in a torn black dress, her hair falling open about her shoulders.*)

SCHIGOLCH: Child, where have you been?—Having your hair curled, I suppose.

ALVA: She does it merely for old memories' sake.

LULU: If only I could use one of you to warm me.

ALVA: Are you embarking upon your pilgrimage barefoot?

SCHIGOLCH: First steps are always accompanied by moaning and groaning. It was the same twenty years ago. And the things she's learned in the meantime! The coals must be fanned a bit first, that's all. After she's been at it a week, a team of horses couldn't keep her in this miserable attic.

ALVA: The bowl's running over.

LULU: What should I do with the water?

ALVA: Pour it out the window.

LULU (*climbs onto a chair and empties the bowl out one of the skylights*): Looks like the rain's finally letting up.

SCHIGOLCH: You ought to be out there now. This is when all the clerks are on their way home after dinner.

LULU: I wish I were lying where nothing could ever wake me.

ALVA: Me, too. Why drag out life when it's like this? Why not die of starvation tonight in peace and oneness. We're at the end of our rope.

LULU: Then why not get us something to eat? You've never earned a cent in your life.

ALVA: You wouldn't turn a dog out on a day like this.

LULU: But *me* you would! You expect me to fill your mouths with the last spark of life left in me.

ALVA: I wouldn't touch a cent of her money!

SCHIGOLCH: Let her go. I'm still longing for a Christmas pudding. Then I'll have had enough.

ALVA: And I long for a beefsteak and a cigarette, and then to die. — I was just dreaming about a cigarette, a cigarette such as was never yet smoked.

SCHIGOLCH: She'd rather see us die here in front of her, than indulge in a little pleasure.

LULU: The people I meet in the streets would rather give me their coats than go with me even for nothing. If you hadn't sold my clothes I wouldn't have to avoid the street lights. I'd like to see the woman who could earn a cent dressed in these rags.

Alva: I did everything humanly possible. As long as I still had money, I spent nights on end figuring out charts that were foolproof against even the most professional card-sharks. And yet, night after night, I lost more money than if I'd poured it out by the basketful. Then I offered my services to the courtesans; but they don't look at you unless you've been stamped by the courts. And besides, they know a gallow-bird when they see one.

Schigolch: True, true.

Alva: I've spared myself no disappointments; but when I cracked a joke, it was me they laughed at; when I appeared as respectable as I actually am, they boxed my ears; and when I tried to be common, they turned so chaste and maidenly my hair stood on end in horror. They have no faith in anyone who hasn't gained the upper hand of human society.

Schigolch: Why not put on your boots now, child? — I don't think I'll grow too much older here. The ends of my toes have been numb for months now. — Sometime around midnight I'll have a few last whiskies in the pub downstairs. Just yesterday the proprietress told me I had a good chance of being her lover.

Lulu: Oh, the hell with it! I'm going down. (*She takes the bottle from the table and puts it to her mouth.*)

Schigolch: So they can smell you coming half an hour away?

Lulu: I'm not drinking it all.

Alva: You're not going down there! You're mine! You're not going down there! I forbid you to go down!

Lulu: Who are you to forbid your wife to do anything, when you can't even feed yourself!

Alva: And whose fault is that! Who but my wife brought me to this miserable, sickly condition!

Lulu: Am *I* sick?

Alva: Who dragged me through the mire? — Who made me my father's murderer?

Lulu: You? Murder *him?* — He was lucky. But seeing you lying there I want to cut off my hands for having sinned so against my judgment! — (*She goes off right, into her room.*)

Alva: She infected me through that Casti-Piani of hers. She hasn't been susceptible to it for a long time now.

SCHIGOLCH: Little devils like her can't learn about suffering too soon — not if they're to become angels in the end.

ALVA: She should have been Empress of Russia. That would have been the right place for her. A second Catherine the Great.

(LULU *reenters from the room with a worn pair of laced boots and sits down on the floor to put them on.*)

LULU: I hope I don't stumble headfirst down the stairs. — Oh, it's so cold outside! —— Is there anything sadder in this world than a lady of pleasure!

SCHIGOLCH: Patience, patience. Wait till business falls into stride.

LULU: I don't care; it doesn't matter about me anymore. (*She puts the bottle to her mouth.*) That'll make me warm — Oh, the hell with it! (*She goes off through the center door.*)

SCHIGOLCH: When we hear her coming we should creep into my cubby-hole.

ALVA: It's a real pity about her. — When I think back — in a way, you know, I grew up with her.

SCHIGOLCH: She'll at least last as long as I will.

ALVA: We went around together at first like brother and sister. Mama was alive then. One morning, just by chance, I came upon her while she was dressing. Doctor Goll had been called into consultation. Her hairdresser had read my first poem that I'd published in *Society*. "Drive your hounds far over the hills; they will return covered with sweat and dust. . ."

SCHIGOLCH: True, true.

ALVA: And then, dressed in rose tulle — with nothing beneath it but a white satin slip — she went to the ball given by the Spanish Ambassador. Doctor Goll seemed to sense his approaching death. He begged me to dance with her so she might be guilty of indiscretion. Meanwhile Papa never once turned his eyes from us, and all through the waltz she looked over my shoulder directly at him. After that she shot him. It's unbelievable.

SCHIGOLCH: I doubt anyone will still bite.

ALVA: Nor would I recommend it.

SCHIGOLCH: The silly fool.

ALVA: At the time, although she was already a fully developed woman, she had the expressiveness of a five year old, happy, very healthy child. And she was only three years younger than me. But how long ago that was. Despite her fantastic superiority in practical matters, she allowed me to explain *Tristan and Isolde* to her. How enchantingly she knew the art of listening.—That little sister, who at her wedding still felt like a school girl, finally developed into the wife of an unhappy, hysterical artist. The artist's wife then became the wife of my dear, departed father. And my father's wife finally became my mistress. That, in short, is the way of the world; against which there is no recourse.

SCHIGOLCH: Let's hope she doesn't run from well-intentioned men and bring up a homeless tramp she's traded hearts' confidences with.

ALVA: The first time I kissed her was in her bridal dress; and afterwards she didn't even remember it. Anyway, I still believe she thought of me while lying in my father's arms. I dare say it can't have been too often. His best days were past. She was always betraying him with coachmen and bootblacks. But when she did give herself to him, it was I who was in her thoughts. And so, she gained this terrible power over me without my even being aware of it.

SCHIGOLCH: They're coming!

(*Heavy footsteps are heard on the stairs.*)

ALVA (*jumping up*): I won't stand for it! I'll throw the bastard out!

SCHIGOLCH (*rises wearily, takes* ALVA *by the collar and shoves him left*): Go on! Go on! How do you expect the poor boy to confess with the two of us wallowing around?

ALVA: And if he asks her to do something common?

SCHIGOLCH: And? And? He's a human being like the rest of us.

ALVA: We'll leave the door ajar.

SCHIGOLCH (*pushing* ALVA *into the cubby-hole*): Nonsense! —Now lie down.

ALVA (*in the cubby-hole*): I'll hear it! Heaven help him!

SCHIGOLCH (*closes the door; from inside*): Shut up!

ALVA (*from inside*): He'd better watch out!

(LULU *opens the door and lets* MR. HUNIDEI *enter.* MR. HUNIDEI *is a giant of a man, with sky-blue eyes and a friendly smile. He wears a cape and tall hat, and carries a dripping umbrella.*)

LULU: This is where I live.

(MR. HUNIDEI *puts his index-finger to his mouth and looks meaningfully at* LULU. *Then he opens his umbrella and places it in the corner to dry.*)

LULU: It isn't exactly comfortable here.

(MR. HUNIDEI *comes downstage and puts his hand over his mouth.*)

LULU: What are you trying to tell me?

(MR. HUNIDEI *puts his hand over her mouth and his index-finger to his own lips.*)

LULU: What's that supposed to mean?

(MR. HUNIDEI *quickly holds her mouth closed.*)

LULU (*breaking from him*): There's no one here. No one can hear us.

(MR. HUNIDEI *puts his index-finger to his lips, shakes his head no, points at* LULU, *opens his mouth as though to speak, points at himself, and then at the door.*)

LULU (*to herself*): Good God — he's a monster.

(MR. HUNIDEI *holds her mouth shut. Then he goes upstage, folds his cape and places it across the chair beside the door. He comes forward with a grinning smile, takes* LULU'*s head in both his hands, and kisses her on the brow.*)

SCHIGOLCH (*behind the half-open door, downstage left*): He must have a screw loose.

ALVA (*behind the door*): He'd better watch out.

SCHIGOLCH (*behind the door*): She sure knows how to pick them.

LULU (*stepping backward*): I hope you'll give me something.

(MR. HUNIDEI *holds her mouth shut and presses a gold piece into her hand.* — LULU *looks at it and tosses it from one hand to the other.* — MR. HUNIDEI *gives her an uncertain quizzical look.*)

LULU: Okay. — That'll do. (*Puts the money in her pocket.*)

(MR. HUNIDEI *leaps madly around the room, waving his arms about, and stares upward in despair.* — LULU *goes carefully to him and kisses him on the mouth.* — MR. HUNIDEI, *laughing silently, quietly, frees himself from her and looks around quizzically.* — LULU *takes the lamp from the flower-stand and opens the door to her room.* — MR. HUNIDEI *enters smiling, raising his hat in the door-way.* — *The stage is dark, except for a ray of light that emerges from the room through the door that is ajar.* — ALVA *and* SCHIGOLCH *creep from their cubby-hole on all fours.*)

ALVA: Are they gone?

SCHIGOLCH (*behind him*): Wait!

ALVA: I don't hear anything.

SCHIGOLCH: We've heard *that* often enough!

ALVA: I'll kneel in front of her door.

SCHIGOLCH: The momma's baby! (*He pushes* ALVA, *gropes across the stage, takes* MR. HUNIDEI'*s cape from the door and goes through the pockets.* — ALVA *has crept to* LULU'*s door.*)

SCHIGOLCH: Gloves — that's all. (*He turns the cape inside out, looks through the inner pockets and pulls out a book which he gives* ALVA.) Look and see what it is.

ALVA (*holds the book in the ray of light emerging from the room and deciphers the title-page with some difficulty*): "Exhortations to Pious Pilgrims and Those Anxious to Become So." — Very helpful! Two shillings, sixpence.

SCHIGOLCH: He seems completely God-forsaken to me. (*Re-*

places the cape on the chair and creeps back to the cubby-hole.) These people are nothing. This country's best days are behind it.

ALVA: Life is never as bad as we imagine. (*He also creeps back to the cubby-hole.*)

SCHIGOLCH: The good-for-nothing bum didn't even have a scarf. And in Germany we grovel on our bellies in front of these people.

ALVA: Come on, let's go back in.

SCHIGOLCH: She thinks about only herself and picks up the first prospect that comes along. I hope the dog remembers her the rest of his life.

(SCHIGOLCH *and* ALVA *creep back into the cubby-hole and close the door behind them.*—LULU *enters and places the lamp on the flower-stand.*)

LULU: Will you come see me again?

(MR. HUNIDEI *holds her mouth shut.*— LULU *looks upward somewhat despairingly and shakes her head.*— MR. HUNIDEI *has thrown his cape around his shoulders and approaches* LULU *with a grinning smile. She throws her arms around his neck, whereupon he gently frees himself, kisses her hand and turns towards the door. She wants to accompany him, but he nods her to remain, and silently leaves the room.*)

(SCHIGOLCH *and* ALVA *enter from the cubby-hole.*)

LULU (*tonelessly*): How exciting he was.

ALVA: How much did he give you?

LULU (*as above*): This. Take it. I'm going back down.

SCHIGOLCH: At this rate we'll be living like princes!

ALVA: He's coming back.

SCHIGOLCH: Let's go back in.

ALVA: He's looking for his prayer-book; here it is. It must have fallen from his cape.

LULU (*listening*): No, it's somebody else. It's not him.

ALVA: Someone's coming up. I hear it quite plainly.

LULU: Someone's knocking at the door now. — Who could it be?

SCHIGOLCH: Obviously a friend he's recommended to us. — Come on!

(COUNTESS GESCHWITZ *enters. She is poorly dressed and carries a rolled up canvas in her hand.*)

GESCHWITZ: If I've come at a bad time, I can leave. I haven't spoken to a soul in the last ten days. I should tell you right away that I didn't get any money. My brother didn't even answer my letter.

SCHIGOLCH: So now madame would like to make herself at home *here?*

LULU (*tonelessly*): I'm going back down.

GESCHWITZ: Dressed like that? — Actually, I haven't come quite empty-handed. I've brought you something else. On the way here, a junk-shop man offered me twelve shillings for it. I couldn't bring myself to part with it. But you can sell it if you want.

SCHIGOLCH: What is it?

ALVA: Let's see. (*He takes the canvas from her and unrolls it, obviously pleased.*) My God, my God, it's Lulu's portrait!

LULU (*crying out*): Monster! What did you bring it *here* for! — Get it out of my sight! Throw it out the window!

ALVA (*as though suddenly renewed, very pleased*): But why? With this around I'll regain my self-respect. It makes my fate seem so understandable. Everything we've lived through is becoming so clear. (*Somewhat elegiacally.*) Let him who feels secure in his bourgeois world when faced with these full, ripe lips, these large, innocent child's eyes, this rosy-white exuberant body — let him cast the first stone.

SCHIGOLCH: We'll have to nail it up. What an excellent impression it will make on our clientele.

ALVA (*very busily*): There's a nail for it over there in the wall.

SCHIGOLCH: How did you come by it?

GESCHWITZ: After you'd left your house I secretly cut it from the wall.

ALVA: Too bad the paint's peeling around the edges. You didn't roll it carefully enough. (*He secures the upper edge of the picture to the nail in the wall.*)

SCHIGOLCH: We need another one down here if it's going to hold. This gives elegance to the whole floor.

ALVA: Let me, I know what I'm doing. (*He removes various nails from the walls, pulls off his left boot, and hammers the nails around the edge of the picture into the wall with his heel.*)

SCHIGOLCH: It'll have to hang there awhile to gain the proper effect. Anyone seeing this will think he's been in an Indian harem.

ALVA (*pulling on his boot and standing up proudly*): Her body was at its peak when this was painted. The lamp, my child! It seems to have grown terribly dark in here.

GESCHWITZ: A very eminent and gifted painter must have painted that.

LULU (*totally composed again; steps in front of the picture with the lamp*): Didn't you know him?

GESCHWITZ: No. That must have been long before my time. I heard you mention he suffered from a persecution mania and cut his throat.

ALVA (*comparing the portrait with* LULU): Despite all she's lived through, the childlike expression in her eyes is still the same. (*Joyously excited.*) But the fresh dew that covered her skin, the fragrant scent of her lips, the radiance that beamed from her alabaster brow, the provocative splendor of the youthful flesh on her neck and arms. . .

SCHIGOLCH: Have all been swept into the dustbin. But she can confidently say: "That's what I once was!" The man whose hands she falls into today can have no conception of what we were in our youth.

ALVA (*cheerfully*): Thank God we aren't aware of this decline when we see those people all the time. (*Lightly.*) A woman is at the height of her beauty when she hurls a man to his destruction. It's her natural destiny.

SCHIGOLCH: Down there in the shimmer of the lights she can hold her own with any dozen spectres of the street. A man who wants to make connections at this hour of the night is more interested in character than physical appearance. He chooses that pair of eyes with the least glint of thievery in them.

LULU (*as pleased as* ALVA): Let's see if you're right about that. Goodbye.

ALVA (*in a sudden rage*): You're not setting foot down there again, as sure as I'm alive!

GESCHWITZ: Where are you going?

ALVA: To bring another one of those bastards up here!

GESCHWITZ: Lulu!

ALVA: She's done it once today already.

GESCHWITZ: Lulu, Lulu, I'll go with you, anywhere, anywhere!

SCHIGOLCH: If you want to sell your own bag of bones, go find your own beat.

GESCHWITZ: Lulu, I won't leave you, not for a moment!

SCHIGOLCH: God damn it! Go fish your own bait!

LULU: You're killing me! I can't bear it!

GESCHWITZ: You have nothing to be afraid of. I'm here with you.

(LULU *goes off through the middle door with* COUNTESS GESCHWITZ.)

SCHIGOLCH: Damn, damn, damn!

ALVA (*throws himself whimpering to his chaise longue*): I think my luck has run its course.

SCHIGOLCH: We should have held that creature back by the throat. That aristocratic death's-head of hers'll scare off anything that breathes.

ALVA: She thrust me onto this sickbed and spiked me inside and out with thorns!

SCHIGOLCH: Yet she has enough guts for ten men.

ALVA: No wounded man ever welcomed a stab of mercy more than I.

SCHIGOLCH: If she hadn't lured that acrobat to my room that time, he'd still be around our necks.

ALVA: He hovers over my head like the bough of golden apples above Tantalus.

SCHIGOLCH (*on his mattress*): — Why don't you turn up the lamp a bit?

ALVA: Can a child of nature suffer as much as all this? — My God, my God, what have I made of my life?

SCHIGOLCH: What's this damnable weather made of my cape? ! — I've known how to take care of myself since I was twenty-five.

ALVA: Not everyone has enjoyed as glorious and sunny a youth as mine.

SCHIGOLCH: I think it's about to go out. — By the time they get here it'll be as dark as a womb in here.

ALVA: With the clearest determination I sought out people who had never read a book. By self-denial and enthusiasm I clung to the basic elements so as to rise to poetic heights. I figured it all wrong. I'm the martyr of my own vocation. Since my father's death I haven't written a single line.

SCHIGOLCH: I hope to God they didn't stay together. — Who but a stupid kid would go home with two women!

ALVA: They didn't stay together.

SCHIGOLCH: I hope not. She'll kick that creature off if she has to.

ALVA: One man, risen from the depths of society, can become the most celebrated person of his nation; the other, born to the purple, can end up in the same depths, unable to die.

SCHIGOLCH: They're coming.

ALVA: And what beautiful hours of mutual, joyous creation they spent together.

SCHIGOLCH: They can do that even better now. — We have to hide again.

ALVA: I'm staying here.

SCHIGOLCH: Why do you pity them anyway? Anybody who spends money, does so with good reason.

ALVA: I haven't the moral courage anymore to be discomfited for a lousy couple pennies. (*He creeps under his rug.*)

SCHIGOLCH: Noblesse oblige! A respectable man acts according to his station in life. (*Hides in his cubby-hole.*)

LULU (*opening the door*): Come in, my sweet!

(KUNGU POTI, *Crown Prince of Uahubee, enters. He is dressed in a light overcoat, light trousers, white spats, yellow buttoned boots, and a gray top hat. Typical African sibilants are heard in his speech which is often interrupted by belching.*)

KUNGU POTI: God damn — is dark on stairs!

LULU: It's lighter in here, my sweet. — (*Pulling him downstage by the hand.*) Come on. Come on.

KUNGU POTI: It cold here. It very cold.

LULU: Would you like a brandy?

KUNGU POTI: Brandy? — Always drink brandy. — Brandy good.

LULU (*gives him the bottle*): I can't seem to find the glass.

KUNGU POTI: It make no difference. (*Puts the bottle to his lips and drinks.*) Brandy. Much brandy.

LULU: You're a very beautiful young man.

KUNGU POTI: My father Emperor of Uahubee. I got six wife here: two Spanish, two English, two French. But — I don't like these wife. I always got to take bath. . . bath, bath, bath. . .

LULU: How much are you going to give me?

KUNGU POTI: Gold piece. — You be sure you will have gold piece. — Gold piece. — Always give gold piece.

LULU: You can give it to me later; but show it to me.

KUNGU POTI: Never pay first.

LULU: But you can at least show it to me.

KUNGU POTI: Not understand. — Not understand. — Come, Ragapsischimulara! (*Takes* LULU *around the waist.*) Come!

LULU (*defends herself with all her strength*): Let me go! Let me go!

(ALVA *has risen tiredly from the bed, creeps up behind* KUNGU POTI *and pulls him back by the collar.*)

KUNGU POTI (*turns around quickly to face* ALVA): Oh! Oh! This den of murderers! — Come, friend, let me put you sleep! (*He hits* ALVA *on the head with a blackjack;* ALVA *sinks groaning to the ground.*) This put you sleep. Good like opium. — You get nice dreams. (*He then kisses* LULU, *and points to* ALVA.) He dream about you, Ragapsischimulara. — Nice dream. — (*Hurrying to the door.*) Here door. (*Off.*)

LULU: I can't stay here! —— Who could possibly stay here now —— I'd rather be down there on the street! — (*Off.*)

(SCHIGOLCH *crawls from his cubby-hole, and bends over* ALVA.)

SCHIGOLCH: Blood! — Alva! —— He has to be put somewhere. — Wake up! — Otherwise our friends might be put off by him. Alva! Alva! — I can't waste time! —— One way or the other; or it'll be too late! —— I'll get him on his feet. (*He strikes a match and sticks it into* ALVA'*s collar.* — *When* ALVA *doesn't move.*) — He wants his peace. — But he can't sleep here. (*He drags him by the neck into* LULU'*s room. Then he tries to turn up the lamp.*) It's about time I left, too, or there won't be any more Christmas pudding downstairs. God knows when they'll be back from their pleasure jaunt. — (*Catching sight of* LULU'*s portrait.*) She doesn't understand the situation. She can't make a living off of love because her life *is* love. — Here she comes! I'll try to work on her conscience. . .

(*The door opens and* COUNTESS GESCHWITZ *enters.*)

SCHIGOLCH: If you want to spend the night here, I suggest you see nothing gets stolen.

GESCHWITZ: How dark it is in here.

SCHIGOLCH: It will be still darker. — The Doctor has already gone to rest.

GESCHWITZ: She sent me on ahead.

SCHIGOLCH: That was wise of her. — If anyone asks for me, I'm in the pub downstairs. — (*Off.*)

GESCHWITZ (*alone*): I'll sit beside the door. I'll watch it all and not move an eyelash. (*She sits down on the cane chair beside the door.*) — People don't know each other — they have no idea what they're like. The only ones who know them are those who aren't human themselves. Every word they utter is untrue, a lie. But they don't know that, because today they're this and tomorrow that, and it all depends on whether or not they've eaten, drunk, and loved. Only the body remains constant for a time, and only children have any understanding. Men and women are like animals; not one of them knows what he's doing. At their happiest moments they moan and groan, and in moments of deepest misery they delight in the slightest trifle. It's amazing how hunger deprives men of the strength to withstand misfortune. But when they've gorged themselves they turn the world into a torture-chamber, and throw lives away to satisfy a whim. — I wonder if there have ever been people who have found happiness in love. — What is happiness to them, but sleeping better and being able to forget everything. — I'm not a human being; my body has nothing in common with human bodies. And yet I have a human soul. The tormented have within them a narrow, shrivelled soul; but I know I have nothing to gain by giving away and sacrificing everything. . .

(LULU *opens the door and* DOCTOR HILTI *enters.* GESCHWITZ *remains unmoving and unseen beside the door.*)

LULU: (*cheerfully*): Come in! Come! — Will you stay here tonight?

HILTI: But I have only five shillings with me; I never leave the house with more.

LULU: Considering it's you, it's enough. You have such honest eyes. —— Come, give me a kiss.

HILTI: God damn it all to hell! Damn! Damn!

LULU: Please, don't!

HILTI: The fact is, this is the first time I've ever been with a woman! Believe me, I thought it would be all quite different.

LULU: Are you married?

HILTI: What the hell makes you think I'm married? — No, I'm a lecturer; I read philosophy at the university. God knows, I come from one of the best families in Basel. All I received for pocket money as a student was two francs, and I used it for better things than girls.

LULU: Is that why you've never been with a woman?

HILTI: Of course! Yes! But I need it now, you see. Just this evening I got engaged to a girl from a very old Basel family. She's a governess here.

LULU: Is your fiancee pretty?

HILTI: Yes, she has two million. — I'm anxious to see what it's like.

LULU (*tossing her hair back*): Lucky girl! (*She rises and takes up the lamp.*) Whenever you're ready, Professor. . . ! (*She leads* DOCTOR HILTI *into her room.*)

GESCHWITZ (*pulls a small black revolver from her pocket, and holds it against her forehead*): . . . Come, come. . . my beloved!

HILTI (*pulls the door open from inside and rushes out*): God Almighty — there's someone lying in there!

LULU (*lamp in hand, holds him by the sleeve*): Stay with me!

HILTI: A dead man! — A corpse!

LULU: Stay with me! Stay with me!

HILTI (*breaking from her*): There's a corpse in there! Merciful God in Heaven!

LULU: Stay with me!

HILTI: How do I get out of here? (*Catching sight of* GESCHWITZ.) And there's the devil!

LULU: Please stop, please!

HILTI: Dirty, dirty, dirty! — My God! (*Goes out through the middle door.*)

LULU: Stay here! Stay here! (*She rushes after him.*)

GESCHWITZ (*alone; lets the revolver sink down*): — Hanging is better. — If she finds me lying in my own blood, she wouldn't shed a tear. I was never more to her than a submissive tool that let itself be used for the most difficult tasks. She abhorred me from the very first, from the very bottom of her soul. — Why not rather jump from the bridge? Which would be colder, the water or her heart? I would dream until I drowned. —— Hanging is better. —— Or perhaps the knife. — Hm, there would be little use in that. —— How often I've dreamed that she was kissing me! And then the next minute an owl taps at my window, and I wake up. —— Hanging is better! No, not the water; water is much too clean for me. (*Suddenly starting up.*) There! — There! There it is! — Quick, before she comes! (*She takes the rug straps from the wall, climbs onto the chair, secures the straps on a hook projecting from the doorpost; places the straps around her neck, kicks the chair away with her foot, and falls to the floor.*) — Damnable life! — Damnable life! —— How can there be more for me! — Let me speak to your heart just once more, my angel! But you're so cold. — I wasn't meant to go yet. Perhaps I'm even to know happiness before that. — Listen to him, Lulu; I wasn't meant to go yet! — (*She drags herself over to* LULU's *portrait, sinks to her knees and folds her hands.*) My adored angel! My love! My star! — Have mercy on me, have mercy on me, have mercy on me!

(LULU *opens the door and* JACK *enters. He is a stocky man, with elastic movements, pale face, enflamed lips, arched and heavy eyebrows, drooping moustache, thin goatee, matted sidewhiskers, and fiery-red hands with gnawed fingernails. His eyes are fixed on the floor. He wears a dark overcoat with a small round felt hat.*)

JACK (*noticing* GESCHWITZ): Who's that?

LULU: That's my sister. She'd mad. I don't know how to get rid of her.

JACK: You have a beautiful mouth.

LULU: I got it from my mother.

JACK: It looks like it. — How much do you want? — I don't have much extra money.

LULU: Wouldn't you like to stay here all night?

JACK: No, I haven't got time. I have to get home.

LULU: Why can't you go home tomorrow and say you missed the last bus and spent the night with a friend.

JACK: How much do you want?

LULU: I'm not asking for piles of gold, but maybe just a — just a small gold coin.

JACK (*turns to the door*): Good night! Good night!

LULU (*holds him back*): No, no! My God, you mustn't go!

JACK (*goes past* GESCHWITZ *and opens the cubby-hole*): Why should I stay here till morning? — Sounds suspicious to me. — The minute I'm asleep you'll roll me.

LULU: No, I wouldn't do a thing like that. I wouldn't do that to anyone. — Don't go away because you think that. Please!

JACK: How much do you want?

LULU: All right, then give me half of what I asked for.

JACK: No, that's too much.—I don't think you've been in the business very long.

LULU: My first day.—(*She pulls* GESCHWITZ, *who is still on her knees and half turned towards* JACK, *by the straps around her neck.*) Now lie down and be quiet!

JACK: Let her alone! That's not your sister. She's in love with you. (*He pats* GESCHWITZ *on the head as if she were a dog.*) Poor creature.

LULU: Why are you staring at me like that all of a sudden?

JACK: I sized you up by your walk. I said to myself: she's really built.

LULU: How can you see a thing like that?

JACK: I even saw you had a pretty mouth.—All I've got on me is a silver piece.

LULU: Oh, what's the difference! Give it to me.

JACK: You'll have to give half of it back, so I can get the bus in the morning.

LULU: I haven't a cent to my name.

JACK: Take another look—every pocket.—Well now, what have we got there? Let's see.

LULU (*holds out her hand to him*): This is all I have.

JACK: Give it to me.

LULU: I'll change it tomorrow morning; then I'll give you half.

JACK: No, I want it all.

LULU (*gives it to him*): For God's sake!—But now come on! (*She takes up the lamp.*)

JACK: We don't need light. . . there's a moon.

LULU (*sets down the lamp*): Whatever you say. (*She throws her arms around his neck.*) I won't hurt you. I love you so much. Don't make me beg you anymore.

JACK: I'm ready. (*He follows her into* SCHIGOLCH'*s cubby-hole.*)

(*The lamp goes out. On the floor beneath the two*

skylight windows are two harsh squares of moon light. Everything in the room is clearly visible.)

GESCHWITZ (*alone; speaks as though in a dream*): This is the last evening I shall spend with these people. — I'll go back to Germany. My mother will send the money. — I'll go to the university. I must fight for women's rights, study law.

LULU (*barefoot, in chemise and petticoat, tears open the door and holds it shut from outside*): Help — Help!

GESCHWITZ (*rushes towards the door, pushing* LULU *behind her, pulls out her revolver and points it at the door.*): Let go! (JACK, *bent double, tears open the door from inside and runs* GESCHWITZ *through with a knife. She fires one shot at the ceiling and crumples up, whimpering.*)

JACK (*tears the revolver from her and throws himself against the outside door*): God damn! I never saw a prettier mouth!

(*Sweat drips from his hair, his hands are bloody. He pants as though his lungs would burst, and stares at the floor with eyes popping out of his head.* — LULU *trembles all over and looks wildly around. She suddenly grabs the bottle, breaks it against the table, and rushes at* JACK *with the jagged neck of the bottle.* — JACK *brings up his right foot and hurtles* LULU *onto her back. Then he lifts her from the floor.*)

LULU: No, no! — Mercy! — Murderer! — Police! — Police!

JACK: Shut up! You're not getting away! Not this time! (*He carries her into the cubby-hole.*)

LULU (*from inside*): No! — No! — No! —— Oh! — Oh. . .

JACK (*reenters after awhile and sets the bowl on the flower-stand*): What a piece! — (*Washing his hands.*) You lucky son-of-a-bitch! (*Looks around for a hand-towel.*) Not even a towel! — Miserable hole! — (*He dries his hands on* GESCHWITZ'*s petticoat.*) This pervert needn't be afraid of me anymore! — (*To* GESCHWITZ.) You won't last too much longer either. (*Goes off through the middle door.*)

GESCHWITZ (*alone*): Lulu — My angel! — Let me see you just once more! — I'm near you — stay near you — forever! (*Her elbows collapse beneath her.*) Damn — damn — da. . . (*She dies.*)

DEATH AND THE DEVIL

A Dance of Death in Three Scenes

CAST OF CHARACTERS

Marquis Casti-Piani
Miss Elfriede von Malchus
Mr. King
Lisiska
Three Girls

A room with curtained windows. Two red upholstered easy chairs facing one another. An ivy screen is set at the edge of both the right and left proscenium so that hiding behind them one may be seen by the audience but unseen by those on stage. Behind each ivy screen is a red upholstered stool. Center and side doors. — ELFRIEDE VON MALCHUS *is seated in one of the upholstered red chairs. It is obvious that she is uncomfortable. She wears a modern dress in the "reformed" style, plus hat, coat and gloves.*

ELFRIEDE: How much longer are they going to make me wait! (*Long pause, during which she sits unmoving.*) How much longer are they going to make me wait! (*Long pause, as above.*) How much longer are they going to make me wait! (*After another pause, she rises, takes off her coat and lays it across one of the upholstered chairs, takes off her hat and places it on the coat. Following this, she paces back and forth twice, obviously agitated.* — *She stands still.*) — How much longer are they going to make me wait!

(*As she finishes,* MARQUIS CASTI-PIANI *enters through the center door. He is a tall man with a bald head and a high forehead; his eyes are large, black and melancholy; his nose powerfully aquiline, and beneath it a heavy, drooping, black moustache. He wears a black frock-coat, dark fancy waistcoat, dark grey trousers, patent leather boots, and a black tie with a diamond pin.*)

CASTI-PIANI (*bowing*): May I help you, Madame?

ELFRIEDE (*excited*): I've already explained to the — lady as clearly as humanly possible why I'm here.

CASTI-PIANI: The — lady told me why you're here, yes. She also told me you're a member of the International Union for the Suppression of White Female Slave Traffic.

ELFRIEDE: I most certainly am! I am indeed a member of the International Union for the Suppression of White Female Slave Traffic. Yet even if I were not, I could not under any circumstance have spared myself this journey. I've been on the trail of this poor unfortunate girl for a full nine months. Till now, everywhere I've traced her to she had just shortly before been carted off to another city. But I know she's in this house! At this very moment! The — lady who was just here told me so in no uncertain terms. She assured me she would bring her to this very room so that I may speak with her privately and undisturbed. I'm waiting here for her now. I have no wish to, nor is there any occasion for me to submit to any further inquisition.

CASTI-PIANI: May I ask you, Madame, not to excite yourself anymore than you are at present. The girl would like to appear in front of you — decently dressed. The lady asked me to tell you this. She feared your excitement might force you into unnecessary violence. But also to make you more at ease waiting in this room.

ELFRIEDE (*walking back and forth excitedly*): You needn't trouble yourself with polite conversation. The atmosphere of this room is nothing new to me. The first time I entered a house like this I had to resist considerable physical discomfort. I realized then the extravagant self-control required of me as a member of the Union for the Suppression of White Female Slave Traffic. Till that time, our efforts had been no more to me than an idle pastime to occupy myself with, so as not to grow old without having done something useful.

CASTI-PIANI: Your remarks wake considerable sympathy in me. Would you honor me with your credentials as a member of the International Union for the Suppression of White Female Slave Traffic. I've learned many persons force their way into this profession only to rescue fallen women. If you're serious in achieving this lofty goal, then you must welcome the control we are forced to exercise in this regard.

ELFRIEDE: I've been a member of our Union for almost three years now. My name is — Miss von Malchus.

CASTI-PIANI: Elfriede von Malchus?

ELFRIEDE: Yes. Elfriede von Malchus. — How do you know my Christian name?

CASTI-PIANI: We do of course read the Union's Annual Report. If I recall correctly, you distinguished yourself as a speaker at last year's annual conference in Cologne.

ELFRIEDE: Unfortunately all I did for two whole years was write and speak, and speak and write, without the courage to come to grips with the traffic itself — and then that same traffic took its toll from under my own roof, from within my own family!

CASTI-PIANI: Unless I'm wrong, it was your own papers, and books, and journals that were to blame — that is to say, you failed to keep them from the hands of the young creature you've now come here to rescue.

ELFRIEDE: You're quite right! I can scarcely deny that. Night after night, satisfied with myself and the world, I lay beneath the covers of my bed for an undisturbed ten-hour sleep never dreaming what was happening; for at the same time, this seventeen year old creature would steal into my study and let her love-starved imagination conjure up out of those piles of books on the campaign the most seductive images of sensual pleasures and appalling vices. And stupid fool that I was, despite my twenty-eight years, I failed to see the next morning that the girl had been up all night. I never in my life experienced a sleepless night. And when I set to work again that morning, it never occurred to me to question the frightful confusion in which I found my papers.

CASTI-PIANI: If I'm not mistaken, my dear Miss von Malchus, the girl had been engaged by your parents for light house duties?

ELFRIEDE: To her own ruination! Yes! Both Mama and Papa were absolutely enchanted by her modest and proper manners. Papa, who is a Civil Servant and a bureaucrat of the first water, considered her presence in the house a veritable ray of light. Following her sudden disappearance, both Papa and Mama no longer spoke of my activity in the Union as spinsterish hysteria, but as an out-and-out crime.

CASTI-PIANI: The girl is the illegitimate child of a washerwoman — is that right? — Do you by any chance know who her father is?

ELFRIEDE: No, I never asked her about that. How do you happen to know all this?

CASTI-PIANI: Hm — the girl read in one of your Union's reports that certain misrepresenting advertisements were published in the daily papers, through which white slave dealers lured young girls into the love market. The next day the girl sought out one of those advertisements, and wrote a very correct letter proposing herself for the position. That's how I became acquainted with her.

ELFRIEDE: How dare you be so cynical with me!

CASTI-PIANI: No, my dear Miss von Malchus — I should rather call it "practical."

ELFRIEDE (*greatly excited, with clenched fists*): Then you're the monster responsible for this girl's disgrace!

CASTI-PIANI (*with a melancholy smile*): My dear young lady, if you realized the cause of your excitement, you might be intelligent enough to keep quiet in front of the monster you think I am.

ELFRIEDE (*curtly*): I don't understand. I don't know what you're trying to say.

CASTI-PIANI: Are you — still — a virgin?

ELFRIEDE (*gasping*): How dare you ask such a question of me!

CASTI-PIANI: What's there to stop me! — But we won't go into that. In any case, you never married. As you've admitted, you're twenty-eight years old. Sufficient proof that in comparison with other women — not to mention the individual you've come here to rescue — you have a very meager degree of sensual awareness.

ELFRIEDE: You may very well be right.

CASTI-PIANI: I say this, assuming the discussion won't annoy you. I consider you neither pathological nor abnormal. Yet are you aware how you've managed to satisfy your sensuality, however weak?

ELFRIEDE: Well?

CASTI-PIANI: By joining the International Union for the Suppression of White Female Slave Traffic.

ELFRIEDE (*with controlled anger*): Just who do you think you are, Sir? — I've come here to rescue a poor, unfortunate creature from the claws of vice! And not to listen to your distasteful lectures!

CASTI-PIANI: Nor did I expect you to. But in this respect, you see, we have more in common than your bourgeois virtue will ever permit you to dream of. Nature has endowed *you* with an extremely limited sensuality. On the other hand, the tempests of life have transformed *me* into a terrible barren wilderness. What the fight *against* the white slave traffic is for *your* sensuality, that *same* slave traffic is for *my* sensuality — assuming you care to concede to me the possession of any such thing.

ELFRIEDE (*enraged*): The hypocrisy of a worthless creature like you! Do you suppose you can silence me with this emotional hocus-pocus? I, who like a weary hound have chased this creature from one den of vice to another? I stand here no longer a member of the Union for the Suppression of White Female Slave Traffic. I stand here a miserable criminal, who without realizing it led a fresh young life into misery and despair. While I live I will enjoy no mouthful of food again, till I snatch that child from destruction. You want me to believe sordid curiosity drove me to this house. Liar! You don't believe your own words! You haven't turned that girl into a marketable commodity out of unsatisfied sensuality — but for money! You've made her a marketable commodity for the sake of a good sale!

Casti-Piani: A good sale! Of course! But good sales are a matter of mutual satisfaction. I never make anything but a good sale. Any other kind would be immoral. — Or do you believe the love market a bad bargain for a woman?

Elfriede: What do you mean?

Casti-Piani: Simply this: — But I don't know if you're in the mood to listen to me attentively.

Elfriede: Will you spare yourself these introductions!

Casti-Piani: Of course. What I mean is this: A man in need often has no alternative but to steal or go hungry. On the other hand, when a woman is in need, she always has the choice of selling her favors. The way is always open to her, for in disposing of her favors a woman need feel nothing. Women have exploited this advantage since the beginning of time. All else aside, man is infinitely superior to woman if only for the pain she suffers in giving birth. . .

Elfriede: Yes, that contradiction cries out to Heaven! I've always said so. Bringing children into the world is anguish and anxiety; and begetting them a pleasant pastime. And yet, beneficent Creation, which has many other idiocies to recommend it, has placed this burden on the weaker sex.

Casti-Piani: And so, my dear young lady, we agree completely on this point. — Yet now you want to deprive your unfortunate sisters of that meager advantage which an — idiotic Creation has thrust upon them: the advantage, in time of need, of selling their favors — a transaction which you would call an indelible disgrace. Fine feminist you are!

Elfriede (*almost crying*): This ability to sell ourselves is not only an inexpressible misfortune, but an eternal curse upon our downtrodden sex.

Casti-Piani: God knows, it certainly isn't *our* fault the love market is a curse of the female sex! We have no more exalted an ideal than that the love market should operate as openly and freely as any other honorable trade! Or that prices in the love market should be as high as possible! If you want to oppose the oppression of your sex, then blame bourgeois society! If you want to defend the natural rights of your sisters, then oppose your own International Union for the Suppression of White Female Slave Traffic!

ELFRIEDE (*flaring up*): I won't listen to any more of your claptrap! I'm convinced that you're not in the least interested in releasing the girl. While I've sat here like a fool, listening to your sociological lecturing, that poor creature has probably been packed off to where she will be forever safe from members of our Union! — Very well, I know my course of action! (*She picks up her coat and hat.*)

CASTI-PIANI (*smiling*): If only you realized how your outburst just now has improved your somewhat rather homely appearance, you wouldn't be in such a hurry to leave.

ELFRIEDE: Let me out of here! It's high time, too!

CASTI-PIANI: Where were you thinking of going?

ELFRIEDE: You know just as well as I where I'm going!

CASTI-PIANI (*grasps her by the throat and cuts off her breathing, at the same time forcing her into one of the armchairs*): You will stay here! There's something else I have to say to you! Go right ahead and scream if you like. We're used to every noise a human can make. So you may scream as loud as you like. (*He lets loose of her.*) I wouldn't be surprised if I make you see reason before I release you and you go running off to the police.

ELFRIEDE (*gasping, tonelessly*): I have never been subjected to such a show of violence.

CASTI-PIANI: How much of your life have you wasted trying to rescue these women of pleasure, as you call them? Why not do something useful for once, such as the promotion of joy! Then you needn't be sorry for the poor creatures anymore. Since the love market has been branded as the most shameful of all professions, women and girls of good society would rather give themselves to a man for nothing than be paid for their favors. And in so doing, these women and girls degrade their own sex in the same way a tailor degrades his trade by making clothes for his customers for nothing.

ELFRIEDE (*as though still dazed*): I don't understand a word you're saying. — I went to school when I was six and stayed there till I was fifteen. I later spent three extra years studying to be a teacher. While I was still a girl, men from the very best of families were invited to my parents' house. I received a marriage proposal from a man who had inherited an estate of twenty square miles, and who would have followed me to the ends of the earth if I had wanted him to. But I didn't feel I could love him. Perhaps I was wrong. Perhaps all I lacked was that small degree of passion which is necessary for any marriage.

CASTI-PIANI: Have you finally been tamed?

ELFRIEDE: Explain just one thing to me: If the life a girl leads here causes her to have a child —— who will look after it?

CASTI-PIANI: You look after it yourself! Or do you as a feminist have something more important to do? As long as there's one woman on God's earth still afraid of becoming a mother, then the emancipation of women will be no more than empty babble. Becoming a mother is as much a necessity of nature as breathing and sleeping. But bourgeois society has barbarically curtailed this inborn right. An illegitimate child is almost as disgraceful as the love market. You're a whore one way or the other. The mother of an illegitimate child is called a whore no less than the girls in this house. If there's one thing in this feminist movement which has sickened me from the start, it's the morality that you've instilled into your disciples for their way through life. Do you really believe that the love market would ever have been denounced as shameful if men had been able to compete in it with women? Professional jealousy! Sheer professional jealousy! Nature has endowed woman with the advantage of being able to do business with her love, and therefore bourgeois society, dominated as it is by men, naturally regards it as the most disgraceful of all crimes.

ELFRIEDE (*rises and takes off her coat which she lays across the chair; walking back and forth*): At the moment I can't say whether your observations are right or wrong. — But how can a man with your education, with your view of society, with your intellectual superiority, spend his life among the most worthless elements of human society! — God knows, it may have been your animal brutality that forced me to take you seriously. And yet I feel certain you've given me things to think of for a long time to come, things I'd never have come upon myself. Every winter now, for years on end, I've listened to some twelve to twenty lectures by every conceivable male and female authority on the subject of feminism. Yet not a single word went so to the heart of the matter as what you've said today.

CASTI-PIANI: We must always be certain that in this life we

are always sleep-walking on the edge of a roof, that any flash of light may make us break our neck.

ELFRIEDE (*staring at him*): What do you mean by that? — Something terrible, I suppose!

CASTI-PIANI (*very quietly*): I said it only in regard to your own views. You've been so certain about them that you've felt free to judge certain matters as "decent" or "worthless." One would think you'd been appointed by God to pass judgment on your fellow man.

ELFRIEDE (*staring at him*): What a great man you are! — What a very *noble* man you are!

CASTI-PIANI: You've just touched a wound which may one day be the death of me. (*He throws himself into one of the armchairs.*) I — am — a — moralist!

ELFRIEDE: And you complain of it? Complain that fate enables you to make others happy? (*Throwing herself at his feet after a short inner struggle.*) In the name of God's mercy, marry me! Before I saw you, giving myself to a man never occurred to me. I've had no experience; I swear by the most sacred of oaths. Till now I had no inkling what the word 'love' could mean. I sense it for the first time here with you. Love lifts man above his unholy self. I'm an ordinary woman — and yet my love for you makes nothing impossible for me. You may go from one crime to the next, but I shall always go before you. Go from prison to the gallows, and I shall always go before you. Please — you mustn't let this opportunity pass! Marry me! Marry me! Marry me! We'll both of us be helped, poor miserable creatures!

CASTI-PIANI (*strokes her head without looking at her*): Whether you love me or not, my child, means nothing to me. — You can't know the thousands of times I've had to allow such emotional outbursts to pass over me. It's not that I underestimate love. But, unfortunately, love must also justify those countless numbers of women who are merely satisfying their sensuality without demanding the slightest compensation for it. And in doing so, they ruin the market for us with their undignified surrender.

ELFRIEDE: Marry me! There's still time for you to begin a new life. Marriage will make an orderly person of you. You can be the editor of a socialist newspaper — you can be a member of the Reichstag. Marry me, and at least once in your life you'll know the superhuman sacrifice a woman's love is capable of.

CASTI-PIANI (*stroking her hair without looking at her*): The best your superhuman sacrifice could do for me is turn my stomach. All my life I've loved tigresses. I was never more than a stick of wood in the company of bitches. My only consolation is that marriage, which you praise so enthusiastically and for which bitches are bred, is a cultural institution. And cultural institutions exist to be overcome. Mankind will overcome marriage as surely as it has overcome slavery. The free love market in which the tigress celebrates her triumph is founded upon an eternal natural law of unchanging creation. And how proud a woman will be when she has won the right to sell herself to the highest bidder without being branded for it. Illegitimate children will then be better off with their mothers than legitimate ones with their fathers. A woman's pride and ambition will no longer be the concern of the man who bestows upon her her position in life, but of the world in which she wins the highest place which her worth makes her capable of winning. What a glorious and fresh sound the expression "woman of pleasure" will then possess! In the story of Paradise it's written that Heaven gave woman the power of seduction. A woman seduces *whom* she wants and *when* she wants. She doesn't wait for love. Bourgeois society defends itself against the infernal danger of our sacred culture by raising its women in artificial intellectual darkness. A developing woman mustn't know what it means to be a woman. State constitutions might come to grief over it. No deception is too common for bourgeois society in its own defense. The love market extends itself with every cultural advance. The more clever the world becomes, the larger the love market grows. Our celebrated culture consigns these millions of women of pleasure to starvation in the name of morality; or else, again in the name of morality, robs them of their honor and the right to live; and still again in the name of morality casts them into the realm of beasts. How much longer must that immorality that cries to Heaven lay waste the world with its executioner's axe of morality!

ELFRIEDE (*whimpering soundlessly*): Marry me! You stand above the world! I offer my hand to a man today for the first time.

CASTI-PIANI (*stroking her hair without looking at her*): Bread and butter culture! Bread and butter culture! — What would the world know of all this morality if man could control love as he does politics?

ELFRIEDE: I want no greater happiness of our love than to spend my life lying at your feet and listening to your words.

CASTI-PIANI (*without looking at her*): Have you ever asked yourself what marriage is?

ELFRIEDE: Till this moment I've never had the cause to. (*Rising.*) Tell me! I'll do anything to meet your requirements.

CASTI-PIANI (*drawing her onto his knee*): Come, my child. I'll explain it all to you. (*When* ELFRIEDE *seems a bit coy for a moment.*) Please sit still.

ELFRIEDE: I've never sat on a man's knee before.

CASTI-PIANI: Give me a kiss. (ELFRIEDE *kisses him.*) Thank you. (*Pushing her away.*) So you want to know what love is. — Tell me who is stronger: a man *with* a dog, or a man *without* a dog.

ELFRIEDE: The man *with* a dog is stronger.

CASTI-PIANI: And now tell me which of these is stronger: a man with *one* dog, or a man with *two* dogs.

ELFRIEDE: I think the man with *one* dog is stronger, because two dogs would become jealous of one another.

CASTI-PIANI: To say the least. But he'd also have to feed two dogs, or they'd run away; whereas one dog could look after itself, and if need be even protect its master against robbers.

ELFRIEDE: Are you using this detestable simile to explain the selfless, indissoluble union between man and wife? My God, the experiences you must have had!

CASTI-PIANI: The man with a wife is stronger economically than the man with none. But he's also stronger than if he had to provide for two or more wives. That's the basis of marriage. No woman, even in dreams, could have hit upon so ingenious an invention.

ELFRIEDE: You poor, pitiable creature! Have you never known the love of a father's house? Didn't you have a mother who looked after you when you were sick, who read you fairy tales while you were recuperating, to whom you could turn when something weighed upon your heart, and who always, always helped you, even when you were certain that nothing in God's world could help you anymore?

CASTI-PIANI: No human creature can experience what I experienced as a child without totally destroying his energy. Imagine yourself into the body of a boy of sixteen who's still beaten for not understanding logarithms! The one who beat me was my father. And I beat him back. I beat my father to death! He died after I'd beat him for the first time. — But those are trifles. You can see the sort of creatures I live among here. Yet never once have I heard them inflict the kind of insults which were my mother's fate all through my childhood, and which every day she would have to challenge with abuse of her own. But those are trifles. The slaps, blows and kicks which my father and mother and a dozen tutors competed with each other for to inflict on my defenseless body were trifles when compared with the slaps, blows and kicks which the vicissitudes of this life have used in their attempt to degrade my defenseless soul.

ELFRIEDE (*kisses him*): If only you could know how deeply I love you for these terrible experiences.

CASTI-PIANI: Life is nothing but death ten times over. Not only for me — but for you. For everyone who lives and breathes. Life for the simple man consists of pain, suffering, and torment which his body must endure. And if he fights his way up to a higher existence in the hope of escaping the body's torments, then his life consists of pain, suffering, and torment which his soul must endure, in comparison to which his body's torments were a pleasure. The horrible fact of life is that man had to conceive of a Being which consisted of nothing but goodness, love, and kindness; and it's to this Being that mankind, in order to be able to endure life, must pray, not only daily, but hourly.

ELFRIEDE (*fondling him*): If you marry me, those torments will come to an end. These problems needn't concern you any further. My Mama has a fortune of sixty thousand Marks. After twenty-five years of happy marriage my Father still knows nothing about it. Aren't you tempted by the prospect of suddenly having sixty thousand Marks at your disposal if you marry me?

CASTI-PIANI (*pushing her away, nervously*): I see you don't understand the art of making love, Miss. You're like a donkey trying to be a lap-dog. Your hands hurt me. That's not from your having learned anything; it's from being a descendant of bourgeois society's inhibited love-life. You have no breeding. None of the necessary sense of delicacy. Sense of delicacy and sense of shame. You lack a feel for the effect of your caresses; a feel which all creatures of breeding are born with.

ELFRIEDE (*jumps up in outrage*): You dare say that to me in this house!

CASTI-PIANI (*having also risen*): Yes, I dare say that to you in this house!

ELFRIEDE: In this house! No sense of delicacy! No sense of shame!

CASTI-PIANI: No sense of delicacy! No sense of shame! I dare tell you that in this house of ill repute! — I suggest you convince yourself with just how much delicacy and tact these creatures carry out their disreputable profession. The least girl in this house knows more about the human soul than the most famous professor of physiology at the most famous university. Of course you, my dear young lady, would experience the same disillusionment here as your past life has conditioned you to experience. I recognize at one glance the woman made for the love-market by virtue of the happy innocence and innocent happiness radiated by her open and harmonious countenance. (*Studying* ELFRIEDE.) In your countenance, my dear, I see neither happiness *nor* innocence.

ELFRIEDE (*hesitantly*): But don't you believe that my industry, my energy, my enthusiasm for all things beautiful can teach me that sense of delicacy and tact?

CASTI-PIANI: No, no, my dear Miss! Certainly not! You may as well forget any such thought.

ELFRIEDE: I'm so convinced of the moral significance of everything you've said, that no sacrifice were too great to overcome my middle-class inadequacy!

CASTI-PIANI: Thank you, I'll have none of it! That would be too horrible! Life is horrible enough! No, no, my dear Miss. You must never so much as lay hands upon the one ray of divine light to penetrate the terrible night of our earthly being! No, no! The one pure flower of Heaven in this sweat and blood stained thicket of our life must not be trampled down by clumsy feet. Believe me, had it not been for this one bright star shining above this howl of anguish evoked by the pains of birth, life, and death, I should have put a bullet through my head half a century ago!

ELFRIEDE: Strain my mind to its limits, I could still never understand you. What is this ray of light that penetrates the terrible night of our being? What is this pure flower of Heaven that mustn't be trampled into dirt?

CASTI-PIANI (*taking* ELFRIEDE *by the hand and whispering secretly*): Sensual pleasure, my dear young lady. Sunny, smiling sensual pleasure. Sensual pleasure is that ray of light, that flower of Heaven, because it is the only serene happiness, the only pure, unmixed joy which earthly existence offers us. Yes, the only thing that has kept me in this world for these fifty years is the selfless worship of this one happiness; its full-throated laughter repays us through the senses for all the torments of our existence!

ELFRIEDE: I think someone's coming.

CASTI-PIANI: Probably Lisiska.

ELFRIEDE: Lisiska? — Who's Lisiska?

CASTI-PIANI: The girl who read those books on White Slave Traffic in your house. You'll see for yourself whether or not I've been boasting. Thank God we're well equipped for such occasions! (*He leads her to the right edge of the proscenium.*) You will take a seat behind this screen of ivy. From here you may observe the pure, unalloyed happiness of two creatures brought together by sensual pleasure.

(ELFRIEDE *sits on the stool behind the ivy screen.* CASTI-PIANI *goes to the center door, looks out, then takes his place behind the ivy screen at the left proscenium.*)

(MR. KING *and* LISISKA *enter through the center door.* MR. KING *is twenty-five years old and dressed in a light-colored knickerbocker-suit.* LISISKA *is dressed in a simple white dress which reaches to the middle of her calves; she wears black stockings, black patent leather shoes, and has a white bow in her loose black hair.*)

MR. KING: I have not come to pass the time with you
As a libertine captivated by your charms.
I shall remain thankful and devoted to you,
If disenchanted I may leave here soon.

LISISKA: You needn't speak so kindly to me.
You're master here; it's you who command.
You needn't fear to paint my bloodless
Face by striking me across the cheeks.
Considering the whore I am
I find that an unheard of gain.
Helpless complaints and whimpering and sobbing
Needn't bother you in the least.
Such pleasant censure is already stale.
Heap torment on torment pitilessly!

If you smashed my face with your fist,
Not even that would satisfy my longing.

MR. KING: I wasn't quite prepared for words like these . . .
Is this a cheerful welcome for your guest —
To hear you talk, you're already burning in Purgatory
In atonement for the pleasures you've enjoyed.

LISISKA: Not at all! Desire, that monstrous beast,
Rages on untamed within my breast.
Do you think that I, a devil's child,
Had ever set foot in this house
If joy could have liberated me
From the terrible beating of my heart?
Joy dries up, a drop
Of water on a hot stone.
And unappeased desire,
A ravening, woeful sight,
Plunges into the abyss
In search of death. ——
Aren't you being cruel then, Sir?
How I regret that!
Why should my chattering bother you
When you strike at me?

MR. KING: If it is really your deep and dark instinct
To climb still farther down from the deepest depths,
Then I should weep, that out of all the stores
Of lovely women I should have chosen you.
I looked in your eyes and my senses were struck with a ray
Of pure, innocent, joyous happiness . . .

LISISKA: Do you want our time to be wasted?
Let it slip by unused?
Down below, Mother Adele
Sits with watch in hand;
Steadily counting and figuring
The minutes of my happiness.

MR. KING: You have been so surfeited with highest bliss,
You long for pain and tears so to exhaust you
Till you are overwhelmed with deep repose,
Which you long for day and night in vain.

LISISKA: If I fall asleep, wake me
With a deep, hard jab in the ribs.

MR. KING: I don't believe you. There's a crack in the mirror.
How is a man to understand that?
Perhaps you dislike happiness and life itself.
But sleep. No. That were blasphemy.

LISISKA: I'm not your property.
You're not my keeper,
So why be afraid of using
My life's properties!
Don't try to comfort my heart
With your humanity!
I have the greatest respect for
The man who beats me unmercifully.
You ask
If I still
Can blush?
Then hit me
And see
How it's done!

MR. KING: Shudders run across my back and chest.
Let me out! I'd hoped, half in ecstasy,
To pluck love's sweet fruit from the tree.
You have offered thorns to me instead.
How can it be that a life as wild as yours
Could stray from the flowered path and be lost in the thicket?

LISISKA: Don't let my desire go
Unappeased!
Don't turn from me heartlessly.
My grave lies open before me.
And I expect to take from this world
As much down with me as possible.
Do you think this craving comes
From being held prisoner in this house?
No! The torturing greed of our senses
Drives us here!
But even *this* reckoning
Was made without reason.
Night after night
I see it revealed as blinding clear as the sun:
That even in this house there is no peace
For the senses.

ELFRIEDE (*with astonishment, from her hiding place*):

Merciful Heaven! This is the very opposite of what I've believed these past ten years!

CASTI-PIANI (*with horror, from his hiding place*): Damn! Damn! Damn! This is the very opposite of what I've believed these past fifty years!

LISISKA: No, you mustn't leave me! Listen to me!
I was an innocent child and began
My life with seriousness, zeal and duty.
Untroubled laughter never became me.
I heard not only my teachers, but my brothers and sisters
Whisper about me in an awesome way;
And even my parents said to me:
One day you'll be the joy of our old age.
Then suddenly the cock crew
And all was past!
Once desire was wakened in me
It grew beyond all bounds
Beyond all thought
Beyond the true feelings of my heart
Until I was amazed at what had happened
At what had made me such a fool
Had made me not see the lightning in Heaven
Nor hear the thunder tumble down from Heaven.
I believed, I hoped that life was given us
For inextinguishable joy!

MR. KING: And didn't you find your hope had been fulfilled?
—I'm speaking, of course, as a blind man speaks of colors . . .

LISISKA:
No — only this infernal urge
That left no room for joy.

MR. KING: And so finally you came to this house,
And here you lead a life of wild abandon.
Music blares, champagne drips from tables,
Laughter roars to waken each new day.
Each long day of work knows nothing more
Than hot tongues whispering of love. —
Ah, what a common beggar I must be
Standing in front of you, proud queen of love!
I came with what was mine, so as to buy

An outright exchange of joy from you.
I could tear my hair with fury now!
Your life is lived in foul pursuit of pleasure!
The libertine's your friend who knows no bounds
Of man's innate restraint to curb his pleasure.
Hurry, then, go deck his limbs with flowers!
I am sustained and cheered by a purer element.
I came here for refreshment: I have no wish
To entangle myself in the filthiest depths of earth.

LISISKA (*imploringly*): No, please stay! — If you leave me now,
Night will come again! Don't go away!
Every word I hear fall from your lips
Is like a whip-stroke goading my desire.
If only you would hate me with such fervor
And strike me with your fists and not your lips
That I could feel each stroke upon my body.
Having once caressed you,
Go back from where you came,
And calmly write my name
Into your note-book, and smile . . .
And I — there still remains for me
The dreadful curse, the infernal urge
That left no room for joy!

MR. KING (*very seriously*): Now I don't trust my senses. It seems to me
You're in love with me. — Oh, what a terrible thing! —
How many dreadful nights I've spent weeping,
Cruelly repulsed by so many women.
Am I now to meet love for the first time
In my life, and from a whore? — Isn't your custom
To give yourself to everyone without question?
And yet you ask for consolation from me!
How eager you are to bare your soul to me,
So that its dark charms can hold me enthralled!
If ever I were placed so close beside you,
The horror of my fate would seize upon me!

LISISKA: For God's sake, you must never trust my love!
My duty here is to pretend at love.
Consider for a moment what it means
When suddenly the door is torn open
And all at once you must scrape your love together:

There stands a man: God created him. —
Would you like for me to begin this dreadful game
With you?
Only to feel disgust at your
Height of bliss?
And yet if with your sturdy peasant's fists
You would chastise my body, and find joy
In doing so, it could bind us together till death.

MR. KING: You are still dressed in robes of innocence.
Not even this terrible house has sullied your soul.
I am blinded by your very purity.
My heart could never tire looking at your image.
Wallowing here in suicide without end
You struggle with your eternally tormented soul,
In face of death and with passionate hate
For all the vain happiness of earth.

(He kneels in front of her.)

Let a friend become a brother to you.
Whether you give your body to me or not
Will remain a secret between us. You've raised me up!
Although I praise these slender knees before me,
You are only mine as soul submits to soul;
And so I am yours too. You'll climb towards Heaven
Out of these hellish torments, and never again
Know the terror of desire flooding over you.
You will resign your life on Heaven's heights.
Humanity will learn of this through me.
Through my chaste verse the world will learn the anguish
Of purchased love, and measure it thereby.
I swear it by the eternal stars of Heaven,
The purest illumination of our night!
Give me a token, tell me in all honesty:
Have you ever found happiness in love?

LISISKA (*raising him up*): If you were to kill me this very moment,
It was never less than this infernal urge
That left no room for joy . . .
And that's how it is in this house.
To all who gather here

Love is eternal torment,
Insatiable greed.
Whatever visitors we have
Are never taken seriously by us.
People like you are rare
Because you don't matter
Like us, always
Compared with the unreasoning beast. —
May I now believe
That you can still this wild
Desire with your kindness?

MR. KING: Whatever tangled paths you lead me through,
There'll always be a star to keep us safe.

LISISKA (*embraces and kisses him*): Come then, my love!
I've made you see at last
How long my dream of highest bliss has been
A land of undisturbed eternal rest! —
If only I could die beneath your fists!

(*Both go off right.*)

CASTI-PIANI (*bursting from his hiding place, as if having seen a ghost*): What were they saying?!

ELFRIEDE (*bursting from her hiding place, passionately*): What were they saying?! Good-for-nothing parasite that I am, what could my withered mind have imagined sensual pleasure to be! — Life in this house is nothing but self-sacrifice and blazing martyrdom! My false conceit, my threadbare self-righteousness made me see this house as a breeding ground of depravity.

CASTI-PIANI: I'm destroyed!

ELFRIEDE: My mouth, that overflowed so with the need for love, with the need *to* love, which was the gift of Heaven itself, all this I've wantonly dragged through the grey soul-stifling filth of the gutter. In my cowardice I saw the sanctity of sensual pleasure as utter indecency.

CASTI-PIANI (*as though having seen a ghost*): That was the blinding flash of light that causes the sleep-walker on the roof to break his neck!

ELFRIEDE (*passionately*): The blinding flash of light!

CASTI-PIANI: What's there left for me when sensual pleasure is only hellish human slaughter, when sensual pleasure is only satanic human slaughter, like all the rest of earth! So this is that ray of divine light that penetrates the dreadful midnight of our martyr's existence! I wish I'd put a bullet through my head fifty years ago! Then I'd have been spared admitting this miserable bankruptcy of my swindling, stolen-together spirituality!

ELFRIEDE: What's there left for you? I can tell you! You're a merchant in women! You're proud of it! You have the best connections of anyone in this traffic. Sell me! I beg of you! Sell me to one of those houses! Oh, the sale you could make with me! I've never loved, I know, but at least that can't detract from my worth. I'll give you no cause to be ashamed of me, no cause to be worried about your honor. I'll swear that with any oath you care to ask of me!

CASTI-PIANI (*half-demented*): What will save me from breaking my neck? What will help me escape this icy shudder of death?

ELFRIEDE: I'll help you. I will. Sell me! Then you'll be saved!

CASTI-PIANI: But who are you?

ELFRIEDE: I want to find death in sensual pleasure! I want to be slaughtered on the blood-altar of sensual love!

CASTI-PIANI: You? You want me to sell you?

ELFRIEDE: I want to die a martyr's death, the same death that young girl who was just here is dying! Haven't I the same human rights as everyone else?

CASTI-PIANI: Heaven save me from this! (*With mounting passion.*) This — this — this is the hellish scornful laughter ringing out over my plunge to death!

ELFRIEDE (*sinks to his knees*): Sell me! Sell me!

CASTI-PIANI: The most terrible times of my life — rising up before me! I once before bartered off a creature in the slave market who was unsuited to it by nature. This crime against nature cost me six long years behind Swedish bars. You can be certain she was one of those characterless creatures whose big feet you can see written in their faces.

ELFRIEDE (*grasping his knees*): I beg you by the very life within me, sell me! You were right! My activity in the Union for the Suppression of White Female Slave Traffic was nothing but unsatisfied sensuality. But my sensuality is not weak! Let me prove it to you! Shall I kiss you as though I were mad?

CASTI-PIANI (*in great despair*): And what of these ear-splitting howls of misery at my feet! What! What of these screams of birth and life and death! I can't bear them anymore! I can't bear these screams of mortal pain and torment!

ELFRIEDE (*wringing her hands*): If you want, I'll even sacrifice my innocence to *you!* If you want, I'll even give you my first night of love!

CASTI-PIANI (*crying out*): The coup de grâce!

(*A shot is heard.* ELFRIEDE *emits a shattering scream.* CASTI-PIANI, *a smoking pistol in his right hand, his left hand clasped convulsively against his breast, staggers to one of the easy chairs and collapses into it.*)

CASTI-PIANI: — Excuse — me — Baroness — I — I — have hurt myself — that — that wasn't — very — polite — of — me —

ELFRIEDE (*has jumped up and bends over him*): No, no, no, you can't have hit yourself!

CASTI-PIANI: Don't — don't scream — like that — in my — ear — be — be — be kind — be kind — if you — if you can —

ELFRIEDE (*recoils in horror, her hands grasping her hair, looking at him, with a scream*): No! No! No! How can I be kind at a time like this! How can I be kind!

(*At the sound of the shot,* THREE SLIM YOUNG GIRLS, *each of them dressed like* LISISKA, *enter curiously, one after the other, from three doors. They hesitantly draw near to* CASTI-PIANI *and look at him, and by means of silent gestures among themselves, they try with great restraint to ease his death struggle.*)

CASTI-PIANI (*looking at the* GIRLS): — Are there — are these — avenging spirits? — avenging spirits? —— No, no! — this — this is — is Maruschka! — I see you so clearly. — This — this is Euphemia! — And Theophila! —— Ma-Ma-Maruschka! Kiss me, Maruschka!

(MARUSCHKA, *the slenderest of the three, bends over him and kisses him on the mouth.*)

CASTI-PIANI (*afraid*): — No, no, no! That was nothing! — Kiss — kiss me differently!

(MARUSCHKA *kisses him again.*)

CASTI-PIANI: — Yes! — Yes! Yes! Yes! — I — I have — deceived you — (*pulling himself up against* MARUSCHKA) — deceived — deceived — all of you! — Sensual pleasure — human torment — human slaughter —— —— at last — at last — release! (*He stands up stiffly, as though convulsed, his eyes wide.*) We — we must — receive our — our gracious Master — standing —— —— —— (*He collapses dead.*)

ELFRIEDE (*finding release in tears, to the* THREE GIRLS): Well? — Hasn't any one of you the courage? You were more to this man than I was ever allowed to be!

(*The* THREE GIRLS, *shaking their heads, draw back coldly, with timidity and fear.*)

ELFRIEDE (*sobbing, turned towards* CASTI-PIANI'S *corpse*): Forgive me, miserable creature that I am. You abhorred me in life from the very depths of your soul. Forgive me for approaching you this last time. (*She kisses him passionately on the mouth; then breaks out in a stream of tears.*) You could not even in your most terrible dreams have conceived of this final disappointment — that in death your eyes would be closed — by a virgin! — (*She closes his eyes and sinks weeping to his feet.*)

BIBLIOGRAPHY OF SELECTED WORKS DEALING WITH THE LIFE AND WORK OF FRANK WEDEKIND

Bernhard Diebold, *Anarchie im Drama* (Frankfurt am Main, 1925).

Hermann Friedmann and Otto Mann, *Expressionismus* (Heidelberg, 1956).

H. F. Garten, *Modern German Drama* (New Jersey, 1959).

Artur Kutscher, *Wedekind: Leben und Werk* (Munich, 1964).

Otto Mann, *Geschichte des deutschen Dramas* (Stuttgart, 1960).

Albert Soergel and Curt Hohoff, *Dichtung und Dichter der Zeit* (Düsseldorf, 1961).